# Net Zeros and Ones

# Net Zeros and Ones

How Data Erasure Promotes
Sustainability, Privacy, and Security

Richard Stiennon
Russ B. Ernst
Fredrik Forslund

WILEY

# About the Authors

**Richard Stiennon** is a renowned cybersecurity industry analyst. He has held executive roles with Gartner, Webroot Software, Fortinet, and Blancco Technology Group. He was a member of the Technical Advisory Committee of the Responsible Recycling standard. He is the author of several books on cyber warfare, as well as *Security Yearbook 2022: A History and Directory of the IT Security Industry*. He has a B.S. in aerospace engineering from the University of Michigan, and an M.A. in War in the Modern World, from King's College, London.

**Russ B. Ernst** has over twenty years' experience in product strategy and management and is frequently sought for comment on issues related to data security in the circular economy. As Chief Technology Officer at Blancco Technology Group, he is responsible for defining, driving and executing the product strategy across the entire Blancco data erasure and device diagnostics product suite.

**Fredrik Forslund** has over 20 years' experience in the data sanitization industry. He is the Director of the International Data Sanitization Consortium (IDSC) and is a sought-after speaker on topics related to IT security and data protection. He is Vice President and General Manager, International at Blancco Technology Group.

# Contents at a Glance

# Contents

# Foreword

I titled my book *If It's Smart, It's Vulnerable* (Wiley, 2022). I first mentioned this fact during one of my talks, and the phrase took on a life of its own. Eventually, it became known as the Hypponen law. When we add functionality and connectivity to everyday devices, they become smart. At the very same time, they become vulnerable and hackable.

This concerns me, because smart devices all contain data. Ensuring that that data does not fall into the wrong hands is the topic of *Net Zeros and Ones*. The right to data erasure here in Europe has been codified in many privacy regulations, including GDPR. But the topic of data sanitization extends well beyond privacy and the handling of personal information.

Security, as the authors point out, is primarily about protecting data from theft, corruption, or even destruction. The last we have seen in many widespread attacks, for example with NotPetya, a worm released on Ukraine by Russia's military. Thousands of organizations have had to deal with ransomware over the last five years. Pernicious criminal gangs have learned to monetize the value we see in our own data by denying us access to it. They encrypt it and demand millions for the decryption keys or to prevent the criminals from leaking the data.

I have spent my career working in cybersecurity. When I started working at the Finnish security company F-Secure in 1991, we did not use the term *cyber*. It was just IT security. The history of this industry is often compared to a cat-and-mouse game between attackers and defenders. I think that metaphor could be expanded: it's a cat-and-mouse game, but the defenders must react to new cats with fresh tactics every year.

When I started, the threat was from so-called hackers who would enjoy demonstrating their prowess in breaking into large organizations or writing malicious code that would spread from machine to machine over the rapidly expanding global Internet. We saw the rise of hacktivists who would target specific organizations in the name of a cause. Cybercriminals arose out of early methods of monetizing access to all these computers. They would commandeer a user's browser to engage in click fraud. They would use password brute-force attacks to steal money and data from online accounts. As the use of computers became ubiquitous and business and governments came to rely on them, state actors used the vulnerabilities in the way these systems were deployed to engage in cyber espionage. Finally, in 2013, Edward Snowden made us all aware of the deep information collection that intelligence agencies engage in, sometimes on a country's own citizens.

Today all of these classes of attackers operate simultaneously, and they continue to evolve their methods and tools. Meanwhile, the defenders scramble to stay at least even with the attackers but often fail, as evidenced by the constant breach and outage announcements we see in the media.

This book offers some small comfort in the fact that for a defender there is an end of the road, at least for one small component of the technology realm— that is when data reaches the end of its useful life. Effective data erasure means that it does not have to be protected by expensive stacks of security appliances in front of the data center. It does not have to be discovered and classified. Access controls are no longer required. Backup and recovery expenses are no more. Encryption, which is a temporal defense, is no longer needed. As computing power grows, it reduces the expense for an attacker who wants to crack encryption keys. Once data is irretrievably erased, it never has to be rekeyed and encrypted.

I mentioned privacy regulations, which are also covered in these pages. Most modern privacy regimes impose strict fines for not taking adequate, even "state-of-the-art" measures to prevent data from being exposed. GDPR Article 17 is titled "The Right to Erasure" and sets out how a data subject can demand that their data be removed from a service such as Google or Facebook. This adds to the benefit of a well-managed data erasure process. In addition to reducing the probability of accidental exposure or outright theft of data, it means the organization can respond to these demands and document that it has complied.

The third element covered in this book is the whole concept of sustainability and the new realm of environmental and social governance (ESG). It turns out that data erasure has its roots as a commercial industry here in Finland. See the story of my friend Kim Väisänen who created one of the primary tools for effective data erasure after his business partner was able to demonstrate how medical records were not properly deleted by local hospitals.

Smart devices, from PCs to tablets to phones to televisions, have a limited useful life. They become obsolete quickly as newer models are introduced. Not only are they expensive to purchase, but vast amounts of raw materials and energy go into manufacturing them. Gone are the days when the only concern with electronic waste was where to put it all.

Electronic waste poses many problems. There are components that can be harmful to soil and groundwater. If they are burned, they can pollute the air. If you are familiar with carbon calculations, you will not be surprised at the amount of carbon released into the atmosphere by the mining of the metals and the refining of the oil that goes into these devices. Then there is the energy expended in the massive factories that churn out the new devices. Add in the packaging, the transportation from the factory, and the delivery vehicles to get a device to your door and you are looking at considerable carbon costs.

An entire industry has arisen to extract value from used electronic gear. IT asset disposition (ITAD) facilities take in the old devices and fix them for resale if possible. If not, they can disassemble phones and laptops to save usable parts for the repair of other devices. An organization can contract with an ITAD to take its old computers and network gear and get the best price. This is money saved for the inevitable upgrade to its IT infrastructure. But what to do about all the data on those devices? This is where data erasure comes into play. ITADs have thrived by getting into the data erasure business. They provide the controls to ensure that all usable data is effectively sanitized from the devices they handle. It turns out that data erasure is a necessary and enabling factor in the reuse and recycling of electronic equipment.

The case is made that these three regimes where data erasure plays a part—privacy, security, and sustainability—justify a systematic data sanitization process. But the authors don't stop with stating their case. They offer guidance on how to fit data sanitization into your data lifecycle management processes.

While reading this book, you will learn all the means used to destroy data from steam rollers to magnetic fields to software. You will learn about the rapid increase in data densities in storage media and the issues that raises. Standards for erasure are evolving too. It turns out that denser storage requires fewer passes of ones and zeros to erase. Forensic analysis of the tracks on a hard drive to discern the ghost images of previous states is no longer easily done. In many ways, solid-state drives (SSD) are even easier to sanitize because they have built-in resets that can flip all the bits to a single state with one command.

The authors also do a good job of highlighting some of the issues with so called crypto-erase, which is the idea that if a hard drive or smartphone is fully encrypted, all you have to do is erase the encryption keys. But you still must check every device to ensure those keys are gone and all the data is encrypted. You can incorporate those checks in your audit practices as part of your data sanitization policy.

One of my favorite chapters contains the stories related by the pioneers of some of the largest ITADs in the world. They each created a healthy business recovering value from millions of used devices a year. They grew from extracting valuable metals from electronic gear to today's modern ITAD service that performs data erasure and fuels the circular economy.

Before the conclusion, the book wraps up with two fun chapters: Chapter 14, "How Not to Destroy Data," and Chapter 15, "The Future of Data Sanitization." Hammers, drills, and nail guns are some of the ways people attempt to make data unavailable. I applaud the awareness of the need to erase data forever but not with a system that means hard drives and computers end up in landfills. The future of data storage ranges from thermal and microwave assistance to decrease magnetic *coercivity* on a platter to DNA storage. The authors offer some ideas on how these future storage devices can be erased.

We are in a battle to protect data from abuse even while the amount of data in the world is growing every day. Spies seek data to discover another nations' intent. Cybercriminals seek to monetize stolen data. Insiders hope to exfiltrate data for their own use or to sell it. The defenders will continue to fight these battles, responding to every new attack by deploying more defenses. Data sanitization is an important tool to minimize the total data attack surface while also gaining compliance with privacy regulations and clawing back value from devices destined for the secondary market.

I encourage anyone who has responsibility for data lifecycle management as well as for securing that data to read this book. It may be the first time you are exposed to the concept of eliminating data at its end of life, or you may be one of the many people who manage data at large organizations. You may have just discovered that there is new regulation working its way through a legislature that is going to impact your business by imposing new controls on how you handle data. This book will prepare you for that day.

—Mikko Hyppönen is the chief research officer at WithSecure and has worked in computer security since 1991. His writing has appeared in the *New York Times*, *Wired*, and *Scientific American*. He has lectured at Oxford, Stanford, and Cambridge and has presented at conferences around the world including at TED in 2011. He is the author of *If It's Smart, It's Vulnerable* (Wiley, 2022).

# Introduction

It has been 27 years since Kim Väisänen and his partner, both in Finland, purchased a hard drive online from a local medical center and discovered thousands of patient records on it. They sent their findings to a journalist who exposed the data leak. The two went on to create one of the first commercial services to reliably erase data from storage devices. Yet, even today, there are very large organizations that get caught disposing of storage media with little concern for the data that resides on them. Or, if they acknowledge the problem, they negligently send the hard drives to be physically shredded in special machines, missing out on the opportunity to do the right thing for both their bottom line and the environment.

In October 2022, ArsTechnica reported the following:

> **"Last month, the US Securities and Exchange Commission fined Morgan Stanley $35 million for an "astonishing" failure to protect customer data, after the bank's decommissioned servers and hard drives were sold on without being properly wiped by an inexperienced company it had contracted."**
>
> ```
> https://arstechnica.com/information-technology/2022/10/
> why-big-tech-shreds-millions-of-storage-devices-it-could-
>                                                      reuse
> ```

There are more than 20,000 data centers around the world today. Many of them upgrade the storage media they use every three to five years as they wear out or as greater speeds and densities are introduced into new models. While many have data sanitization polices in place to completely wipe these devices before they leave the premises, many do not.

Microsoft Azure's practice is reported to be to physically shred hard drives in its 200+ data centers "to protect customer data." The following is from the same ArsTechnica article:

---

**"Microsoft says 'we currently shred all [data-bearing devices] to ensure customer data privacy is maintained fully.'"**

---

Also in October, the *Financial Times* ran a story about tens of thousands of devices being needlessly shredded. "From a data security perspective, you do not need to shred," says Felice Alfieri, a European Commission official who co-authored a report about how to make data centers more sustainable and is promoting data deletion over device destruction.

So yes, Microsoft and others understand the privacy and security concerns covered in this book, but they completely miss the opportunity to safely sanitize storage to avoid shredding devices that end up as landfill or are incinerated—contributing to air pollution.

Sustainability is becoming a primary driver for using good data sanitization procedures. Certified IT asset disposition (ITAD) services started as a business that recovered valuable minerals—gold, silver, rare earths—from printed circuit boards. They have evolved, spurred by numerous regulations, into a service that extracts residual value from old equipment. They refurbish cell phones, laptops, and desktops for resale. Those devices that cannot be repaired are dissembled so their component parts can be used in the repair process. Thanks to customers who recognize the data security issues of sending their devices to a third party, ITADs started to offer data sanitization and tracking so that a customer would have a record of every device that had been sanitized. You will learn in Chapter 9 how three of the top ITADs in their respective regions have started to see their customers leverage responsible recycling as part of their environmental and social governance (ESG) programs. It is even possible to project what carbon/energy savings are created when a device is reused instead of being trashed.

There is growing momentum for data sanitization across all industries. This can be seen in new standards being written to expand on older standards. This book will bring you up-to-date on the standards for data sanitization and new standards being written. Keep in mind that where standards lead, regulations are not far behind. Rather than define proper practices in a new law or regulation, the creators often defer to the standards.

If you are just embarking on a data sanitization project, this book will guide you in creating a data sanitization policy that fits in with your information lifecycle policies. A suggested policy is included in the Appendix.

You would think that encrypting data at rest would be the final solution to the problem of data leaks. Modern encryption algorithms are breakable only (theoretically) by the major intelligence agencies. Yet, encryption fails all the time. A self-encrypting drive may be misconfigured when it is shipped so that encryption is not turned on. A factory reset on most phones is meant to destroy the encryption keys and render all the data unreadable. Yet, the phone may connect to a cloud backup and recover its own keys! The greatest benefit of so-called crypto-erase is that it is much faster than the logical erase procedures required to overwrite zeros and ones. The critical factor is to determine that the encryption keys have truly been erased and that the storage media is encrypted.

If you are a data center operator, you can extract tremendous value from a data sanitization program. Your data security policies may prevent you from taking advantage of hardware warranties, forcing you to pay for replacement hard drives instead of getting them replaced as part of a returned material allowance (RMA) program. If you erase those hard drives with an auditable, verifiable process, you can save significant expense.

RSAC, the organizers of the largest cybersecurity conference, estimate that there are three million cybersecurity professionals. All of them, regardless of their specialization in network, endpoint, identity, or cloud, are ultimately responsible for data security. Their task is to prevent data from being stolen by cybercriminals, spy agencies, or even malicious insiders. This book offers relief in a small but important way. At the end of data's useful life, it can be completely erased forever, removing the need to discover it, track it, and protect it. It changes the organization's task from "protect all data forever" to "protect all data for seven years," or whatever the regulatory requirement dictates.

This book on data sanitization is meant to be a single resource to promote good privacy and security while providing a path to a more sustainable existence. Rather than slow the progression of technology, data sanitization provides a path to accelerate technology adoption while extracting value from older devices.

It is hard to estimate how many old devices clutter up the homes and storage closets of consumers and businesses. Just count how many old phones and laptops or tower computers you keep around. As sanitization methods, services, and tools become more widely available, these devices could at least be responsibly disposed of.

The speed at which data is being created and accumulated is starting to highlight the need for data management to curtail costs. Assigning an expiration date to data is one of the most impactful steps to reduce storage costs while complying with strict data retention regulations. The expiration date is the trigger to sanitize the data according to policy.

Perhaps this book will get into the hands of the engineers and scientists working on new ways to store and retrieve data. The hope is that they will take into consideration the data sanitization requirements, thus preventing a new wave of devices that pose a data security threat.

Sustainability has its part to play too. ESG regulations are requiring the "right to repair" and imposing new guidance on recycling. Both of these need data sanitization to be effective. Just as privacy regulations intersect with cybersecurity requirements, ESG touches on information technology practices. Thus, all three—privacy, security, and sustainability—have their part to play in driving data sanitization forward.

Use this book to guide your own data sanitization practices. If you are just starting out, you can use the information contained here to build a case to create a data sanitization policy and start implementing practices that ensure your data is responsibly disposed of on a regular schedule.

# End of Life for Data

Data is like water. It seeps into everything and pours out of every process and device. Every single minute of every day, we create data. Even while we are sleeping, our bank, insurance company, mobile phone, or wristwatch is ticking away, creating records of transactions, our location, our heart rate, even our sleeping patterns. When we are awake, we are creating data in spreadsheets, documents, and every application we interact with online. This book is about finding and erasing data at the end of its useful life, no matter where it is hiding.

There are many reasons to erase data. Preserving privacy is one of them. Your personal records are yours and should not belong to Google or Facebook, even though those companies track your every move online and record it. What about all the data on an old cell phone or computer that you are selling online? How do you ensure everything is securely erased from those devices? Do you connect your phone to a rental car's infotainment system to play your favorite songs or make it easy to call a contact? How do you erase that data from the car when you return it? Do you know where all the logs of your activity are stored?

Security is another reason. The purpose of cybersecurity tools, from firewalls to analytics to endpoint protection, is to protect data. Data sanitization is the ultimate protection from theft, breach, or leakage of critical data.

In recent years, the ideas of sustainability and environmental and social governance (ESG) have led to another use case for data sanitization that is growing in importance. By certifiably removing all data from a device, it is now possible to funnel those devices into a circular economy where they can be refurbished, resold, and reused. The value extracted from used devices often pays for the processes to erase data from them and recycle those components that are beyond repair. The value returned to the owner helps reduce the total lifecycle cost of owning a cell phone or computer.

In addition to management of your personal data, this book is a guide to creating and executing a complete corporate data erasure program. If you are responsible for your company's data management, you already know about data retention policies, which may be different in every country your company operates in. A data retention policy implies that you have a process for destroying data at the end of its life. You certainly need to ensure that all data is completely destroyed when you dispose of outdated laptops, desktops, servers, network gear, storage arrays, magnetic tapes, and loose hard drives.

Data sanitization is the last and profoundly final step in a data protection plan. Throughout the life of data, the goal is to protect its confidentiality, integrity, and availability. When that data is no longer needed, the task is to irrevocably wipe it. This removes the need for confidentiality and integrity, and it is assuredly not available. This end of life for data is profound because it represents one of the only aspects of IT security that is truly final. The burden of deploying firewalls, intrusion prevention systems (IPSs), data leak prevention (DLP), access controls, authorizations, logging, auditing, and encryption is finally over, never to cross a chief information security officer's mind again. Gone are the risks of accidental exposure in the cloud, of a lost or stolen laptop or smartphone, of ransomware, of identity theft, and being in violation of regulations like the EU General Data Protection Regulation (GDPR) or the California Privacy Rights and Enforcement Act of 2020 (CPRA), which takes effect January 1, 2023.

In recent years, sustainability and ESG have come into play. Many large companies tout their targets for lowering carbon emissions and getting to a "net zero" carbon footprint. In a 2020 press release, Apple committed to become carbon neutral across its entire business, manufacturing supply chain, and product lifecycle by 2030. Data sanitization plays an important role here because reusing electronic equipment, be it desktops, laptops, cell phones, tablets, or office equipment, is a key way to reduce a carbon footprint. Companies can account for the carbon savings from a reused laptop that can offset the total carbon in terms of material, energy, and transportation that goes into creating a new one.

*Data sanitization* is the term used to define the organized and certified destruction of data. It could be for a full disk, either a hard drive with its spinning disks or silicon solid-state drives (SSDs). It could be for USB thumb drives, magnetic tapes, medical devices, network gear, an entire data center, a cloud image, or the device used to generate and store nuclear launch codes. Other terms used throughout this book are data erasure, wiping, destruction, or overwriting. As we will see, data sanitization is the specific term used when a program, driven by policy, is used to accomplish the complete removal of data from physical storage or memory with a documented procedure suitable for auditing.

Technologies used to accomplish data sanitization include overwriting with various schemes of 1s and 0s, resetting flash memory storage, erasing strong encryption keys, destruction by magnetic fields (degaussing), incinerating, and physical shredding. While drilling through a hard drive case and the enclosed platters is probably the most cited method for home use, there are machines available for mangling hard drives and pulverizing SSD cards called *shredders*.

When sanitizing data, there is a concept of provenance. Who controls the data as it passes out of use and is ultimately destroyed? If you send a hard drive or computer to an IT asset disposition (ITAD) facility for recycling, when do you get assurance the data cannot be recovered from the devices? In your own facility? When they are received at the ITAD? Before they are refurbished and sold as used? The National Security Agency (NSA), which is understandably the agency that is most aware of the value of lost or stolen data, uses a belt and suspender approach; it degausses devices before physically shredding them. What should you do? What are today's technology options to combine total security and circularity? These questions and more will be answered as you continue reading.

## 1.1    Growth of Data

If, as Marc Andreeson said in a 2011 *Wall Street Journal* op-ed, "software is eating the world," then surely the world is being drowned in data. IDC estimates that what they call the *global datasphere* will grow from 33 zettabytes (ZB) in 2018 to 175 ZB by 2025. A zettabyte is 1,000 petabytes. A petabyte is 1,000 terabytes. Each terabyte is 1,000 gigabytes. YouTube alone contains 1.4 ZB of video. Think of the 1.3 million laptops and PCs sold every year. How much data is on the computers these are replacing? Think of the billions of smartphones in use around the world. How many photos and videos are being created every day? Think of the data being created every time you accept a cookie as you browse the web. The logs in each web server are recording your IP address and your session and, yes, the cookies that reside in your browser. Now think of the cloud—all the servers, data buckets, virtual machines, virtual private clouds (VPCs), containers, data lakes, and apps that are generating or storing data every second. Then contemplate the 20 billion Internet of Things (IoT) devices—cars, cameras, and industrial sensors—that are recording and storing data. On top of that are the logs of every single transaction, the network traffic recorded, the medical information, the movement of stock prices, and every bid and ask price.

While the value of a single datum may be minuscule, in aggregate, data miners are using so-called big data to extract intelligence from vast quantities of data stored in "data lakes." The idea that data could be of value at some future date encourages governments and tech giants such as Google, Apple, Amazon, Twitter, and Facebook to store everything forever.

The cost of storage is plummeting. A storage device 50 years ago cost tens of thousands of dollars and had a capacity measured in single-digit megabytes. Today a hard drive in a storage array is typically multiple terabytes and costs less than $1,000.

## 1.2   Managing Data

Luckily, storage is not free. Cloud storage, while plummeting, still has a significant cost: $23/month for a terabyte in Amazon S3, for instance. That means data has to be managed. In addition to cost, the elements of data management include discovery, classification, and risk scoring. All data deemed critical should also be backed up and easy to recover if the original data is corrupted. Data backup creates more data, compounding the data management task.

### 1.2.1   Discovery

Data discovery is the first, and most difficult, task. There are many tools available for data discovery. The first task is to know where all of an organization's data resides. Servers, desktops, mobile devices, network attached storage (NAS), backup and recovery systems, tape archives, cloud storage, and thumb drives may be the physical location. But there are more places data resides such as the active memory in servers and desktops or cloud workloads. And of course, multiple third parties may have your data.

## 1.2.2 Classification

Once an organization's data is found, classification is required to determine the following:

- Its importance to business operations. There is a difference between data collected from a remote temperature sensor and financial transactions, for instance.

- The likelihood that the data will be of value to a competitor or cybercriminal.

- Any regulatory compliance requirements.

- The data retention timeframe for the data based on the laws of the country it resides in, and the regulations that the organization must comply with.

- Whether the data is part of an ediscovery process initiated by a party to a lawsuit or a regulator and therefore on legal hold.

Intelligence agencies are known for their strict data classification policies. From For Official Use Only (FOUO) to Top Secret or Five Eyes Only (FEO), they tend to err on the side of over-classification.

Most organizations use laws and regulations to guide their data classification. They may include personally identifiable information (PII) such as name, email, address, national identity number, and health records. Other data that may fall under specific regulations:

- Financial records
- Credentials
- Intellectual property

(The term *personally identifiable information* is being displaced by *personal information* in new regulations.) Many organizations start with identifying the "crown jewels"—the data that must be protected at all costs such as Coke's legendary "secret formula" or Pratt and Whitney's newest jet engine design, for instance. Many attempt to classify all of their data. This may be an insurmountable task. How do you classify an email, PowerPoint presentation, spreadsheet, or transcript from a Teams or Slack channel? One approach is to take into account the role of the person who created the data. A spreadsheet created by the CFO may be deemed more critical than a to-do list created by a graphic designer. Data that falls under a particular regulatory regime is often the simplest to identify and classify: credit card numbers for PCI DSS, account information for Gramm Leach Bliley, health information for HIPAA, and PII for GDPR.

If you think about it, all of the 3,050 vendors that make up the cybersecurity industry provide solutions that, ultimately, protect data. The Data Security category alone contains 398 vendors that exist to most directly protect data. The solutions include encryption, key management, public key infrastructure (PKI), digital certificates, secure communications, secure file sharing, data discovery, and classification. But, because an attacker is trying to either steal data, corrupt data, or deny access to data (attacks against confidentiality, integrity, and availability [CIA]), all of the other vendors' solutions exist to protect data too. The 366 Network Security vendors tracked by Stiennon are there to protect data as are the Endpoint Security solutions (229 vendors), Identity and Access Management (380), and the Governance Risk and Compliance (GRC) vendors (412).

Ironically, the traditional meaning of *data protection* was to make data as reliably *available* as possible. Immutable (read-only) data storage, RAID systems, backup solutions, disaster recovery, and redundant data centers all make the job of data sanitization at the end of life for data more complicated.

### 1.2.3   Risk

Measuring risk to data is also hard to do. The following are contributing factors:

- **Value**: At the very least, how much would it cost to re-create the data? At the top end, what cost to the business would arise if that data were unavailable or stolen?

- **Targeting**: Defense contractors, government agencies, and even nongovernment organizations (NGOs) such as think tanks have to worry about espionage. Just about every organization has to worry about cybercriminals who may be after credit cards and bank accounts or just seek to encrypt all of your data and hold it ransom.

- **Exposure**: Is the data on an Internet-facing resource? Is it on a widely shared server within the organization? Is it on a laptop that could be stolen from a car or employee residence?

## 1.3   Data Loss

Data loss can be inadvertent, accidental, or the result of data theft. Examples of inadvertent data loss include the myriad times data is stored in a cloud bucket that is discovered by researchers who scan systems like Amazon S3 for large stores of data. These researchers usually notify the data owner so they can take steps to correct the access configurations and put controls in place. But then the researchers publish the exposure, often misidentified as a data breach by the press. It is always bad to be the subject of such exposure because without proper controls in place the possibility always exists that the researcher was not the only one to discover the misconfiguration.

### 1.3.1    Accidental

Accidental data loss can occur when a critical document, spreadsheet, or file is sent to the wrong recipient. These can be embarrassing if the recipient is a journalist or blogger. They can be devastating if the data loss involves confidential medical or financial records. Often data loss occurs when a laptop, desktop, or server is stolen. The thief is typically interested in the equipment and not the data, but the loss can be as impactful as a targeted data breach and incur all the same costs. Breach notification laws may require that every person whose data was included in the loss has to be notified. There may be fines associated with the loss. In 2006 a burglar broke into the home of a data analyst who worked for the U.S. Department of Veteran Affairs (VA) and stole the analyst's laptop. It contained the records of 26.5 million U.S. veterans. This set off a massive effort on the part of the VA to install full disk encryption (FDE) software on all of its computers. The laptop was later recovered when it was sold near a subway station in Wheaton outside of Washington DC. The buyer saw published notices and turned it in.

Another path to accidental data loss is improperly disposed of computers or hard drives. Cybercriminals and researchers have been known to purchase these from eBay to see what information still resides on them. As we will see, one such case occurred in Finland and led to the beginnings of the data erasure industry.

### 1.3.2    Theft

A cybercriminal, hacktivist, competitor, or nation-state could steal your data. Cases of data theft abound: Titan Rain in 2003, when Chinese spies infiltrated U.S. government research labs; the theft of clearance applications from the U.S. Office of Personnel Management; the theft of design data from the Defense Industrial Base (DIB) discovered in 2008. Since 2009, shortly after the invention of crypto currencies, ransomware has become one of the greatest threats to data. An attacker gains a foothold within a target organization, deploys one of many families of ransomware, and proceeds to encrypt the data and hold the encryption keys for ransom. Over the last several years cybercriminals like the Conti hacking group with hundreds of employees have also exfiltrated the data, so they have the additional leverage gained by threatening to publish the data if the victim does not pay up.

An interesting case from 2020 involved a large nonprofit organization. A threat intelligence team led by now famous ransomware negotiator, Kurtis Minder, was browsing the cybercriminal forums where attackers sell access to compromised networks (technical term: *initial access brokers*). From the data revealed, the researchers could figure out which organization it was and reached out to them to give them a heads up that their networks had been compromised. The nonprofit verified that it was under attack and proceeded to lock down its networks to stop the attack. Unfortunately, a significant portion of the data was already being systematically encrypted. The organization engaged Minder to help deal with the attacker who was demanding millions of dollars to provide the decryption keys. More important, the cybercriminal also verified that he had stolen the data and threatened to publish it if the nonprofit did not pay the ransom.

Like a case of kidnapping when the negotiator asks for proof of life, a ransomware negotiator asks for proof of data. The attacker gave Minder access to the file server that contained all of the purloined data. But the connection speed was extremely slow, too slow to allow Minder to just retrieve all of the data. Luckily, the nonprofit had backups of most of its data. It is typically a lot faster to restore from backup than it is to decrypt full file systems. The one element that was not backed up was the real-time records of configurations for the organization's cloud infrastructure. These are small files, and Minder's team was able to re-exfiltrate them from the attacker's repository! Two lessons learned:

- You will never be able to identify all of the data that is critical to your operations.
- You should back up everything.

A similar story is told by Andy Greenberg of *Wired* magazine. Notpetya was the most damaging cyber incident ever. A worm released through an update for a Ukrainian accounting software company, M.E.Doc, spread to thousands of companies around the world. One of the hardest hit was giant shipping company Maersk, which claimed hundreds of millions of dollars of losses. Notpetya masqueraded as ransomware, leaving a message that all files had been encrypted and to pay a ransom to recover them. In reality, the data was completely destroyed and was unrecoverable (perhaps they used crypto-erase?). Maersk's shipping and ports were shut down for nine days as the company recovered from backups. The one set of data they did not have was a current copy of an Active Directory domain controller. Luckily, one domain controller in Africa had been taken out of service prior to the attack and was still clean. Maersk flew an employee to Africa where he picked up the hard drive containing the critical files and carried it back to headquarters. Note, yet again, the same lessons learned: have backups of everything, and you never know what is *critical* data.

### 1.3.3   Dumpster Diving

In the early days of hacking, it was not uncommon for hackers to rifle through the trash of a target organization looking for clues to assist them in their attacks. In his 2008 book *No Tech Hacking*, Johnny Long describes the wealth of data a hacker can recover from looking at trash, from network diagrams to usernames and passwords to job positions. This includes names and phone numbers of employees, email addresses, bank accounts, names of servers, anything that provided details. Identity thieves will steal trash bags off curbs looking for bills and other documents containing personal information. Discarded computers, thumb drives, and CDs are also rich sources of data that should be kept away from dumpsters. Besides, there are much more responsible ways to dispose of hardware.

## 1.4   Encryption

Encrypting data is the best way to protect against data loss. Requiring that all data be encrypted everywhere all the time means that a loss of a device, file, or disk drive will only incur inconvenience and minor costs to replace the device. California's breach notification laws explicitly state that breach notification is *not* required if stolen or lost data is encrypted, although CA 1386 does not specify the strength of encryption. Other U.S. state laws do. The assumption is that the attackers will not have access to the encryption keys to decrypt the data. The keys should not be easily recovered from the device. On a cell phone, the keys are accessed with a four-digit pin; thus, additional protections are usually deployed to erase the keys if there are too many attempts to unlock the phone.

Modern encryption relies on strong algorithms and long keys to ensure that even the NSA would have difficulty decrypting the data. Because it is so expensive to crack a key, attackers look for ways to compromise the keys themselves. Thus, key management is required to issue keys, revoke them when necessary (when an employee leaves an organization for instance), and re-key devices when they change hands or the algorithms have to be updated.

## 1.5   Data Discovery

There are three primary drivers for establishing a data discovery process: regulations, security, and preparing for legal discovery (or *ediscovery*). As organizations grow and adopt new technology platforms, it is not unusual for them to have a wide-ranging mix of legacy and new technology. This means a data management platform must span multiple infrastructures: the mainframe with its massive storage as well as the cloud instances of database as a service (DBaaS), the data lakes used to train artificial intelligence models, the backup and recovery systems in multiple data centers and across multiple cloud regions. It is unlikely to find a tool that can discover and identify data across all platforms, so managing multiple tools may be required.

## 1.6    Regulations

The GDPR is the world's most extensive privacy legislation. One of its tenants is data discovery and identification of all data on EU residents, termed *data subjects* in the regulation. The political process to arrive at the GDPR was extensive. Since the 1990s there have been discussions, debates, and different initiatives that finally led to the approval and implementation of the new legislation regulating the use and management of PII. Personally identifiable information can include names, addresses, email, phone numbers, national identity numbers, IP addresses, browsing behavior, and medical records. Discovering these data stores is the first step to compliance with the rest of GDPR, which requires that "state-of-the-art" security be used to protect data from misuse or theft. The regulation also extends to any third parties that may be processing the data. For the purposes of GDPR and other privacy regulations (CPRA, GLB, HIPAA, and PCI, in the United States), a data management program should do the following:

- Identify every system that stores personal information and what that data is.
- Identify every location where personal information resides.
- Establish a policy to control who has access to the personal information.
- Identify the systems that can read and write to the personal information data stores and establish controls for the systems.

One essential way to reduce the burden of regulatory compliance is to reduce the amount of data collected and stored. Only data required for business operations should be managed. By effectively erasing unneeded data, the burden of management is reduced. So is the exposure to regulatory oversight.

## 1.7    Security

Many organizations architect their security programs in concentric circles of defense. They often draw the series of rings in this order: network, endpoint, data. Since data is the most fluid component, they often fail to protect it everywhere, so they embark on a program to identify the "crown jewels," the most important data that represents both the greatest value to the organizations as well as the greatest potential damage if it is lost or stolen. The crown jewels may be the most closely held intellectual property like design data for their primary manufactured product, financials, and plans for mergers, or, in a consumer retailer, customer data.

The exercise to identify crown jewels requires data discovery with the additional step of scoring the value of that data, or the risk associated with losing the data. Once data is assigned the rank of most important to protect, the organization invests in the technology and processes to defend it. It may be segregated to the data center and never put in the cloud. It may be put on its own subnet so connections to the data are denied unless explicitly allowed. It may be encrypted and strong multifactor access controls put in place. Effective encryption implies effective key management. Of course, encryption keys themselves should be considered crown jewels.

Part of the fallout from an exercise to identify crown jewels will be the classification of data on the other end of the spectrum: data that is not valuable at all, or is valuable for only a short time. This can help identify data that should be sanitized, removing all danger that it will ever be part of a breach.

## 1.8  Legal Discovery

During a regulatory action or a civil suit, parties demand copies of all pertinent records, often cast with a wide net. The field of ediscovery is dedicated to managing this process. Large organizations may be subject to many lawsuits with discovery actions at the same time. The process starts when the aggrieved party sends a hold notification to sequester all relevant data. That data must be collected in a form that can be made available to the suing party. There was a time that meant creating physical copies of memos, documents, emails, and records. Today it also includes electronic data. Ediscovery tools are needed to provide the minimum data while preventing the disposal of requested data to avoid any accusations of destruction of evidence, or *spoliation* to use the legal term.

These legal processes introduce the concept of data retention periods. Laws, regulations, and sometimes "common practice" are used to set time limits on data retention. They vary for each type of data. For instance, bank statements and financial records may be limited to seven years. Office documents like slide decks could be assigned a retention period that is shorter, say, three years. Every country may have different legally required retention periods. A global company may have hundreds of different retention rules for hundreds of different data types. That's why a robust data management program is needed.

The U.S. State Department's data retention policies were under the spotlight during the 2016 Presidential election. One candidate, the former Secretary of

State, used data sanitization tools to remove email from her personal equipment. The State Department's data retention policy is public. While the Secretary of State is in office, all correspondence, documents, schedules, everything, are kept. After the Secretary leaves office, they are moved to a records office for a time, and after that period they are handed over to the National Archives to be kept *forever*. The only data singled out for disposal is invitations to events that the Secretary declined. Everything else is kept.

The best practice is to do the following:

- Assign a retention period to all structured and unstructured data (for structured, think databases or spreadsheets; for unstructured, think documents, emails, slide decks, videos, chats, etc.).
- Schedule all "expired" data for sanitization.

As shown, data management is required for regulatory, security, and legal actions. As data continues to grow exponentially, so do the inherent risks associated with the data. Sanitizing unneeded data in a timely way will reduce exposure to risks in all three areas. It will also help contain storage costs and other expenses connected to the waste of managing and securing all of that data.

## 1.9   Data Sanitization

As mentioned earlier, there are many ways to destroy data. They include physical destruction of the media data is written on (tapes, hard drives, SSDs, thumb drives, paper) and various methods of overwriting the data so it is not able to be recovered.

Data sanitization is the process of deliberately and irreversibly removing or destroying the data stored on a memory device to make it unrecoverable. A device that has been sanitized has no usable residual data, and even with the assistance of advanced forensic tools, the data will not ever be recovered.

Any data destruction has to fit within an auditable process. The scheduling of data sanitization for devices, files, and databases should be driven by the regulatory, security, and legal procedures mentioned earlier. Once data has been irreversibly removed or the device destroyed, there should be a record kept of the procedure. Data erasure software should report on the successful overwriting of all the sectors on the disk or the wiping of data from any memory chips that are part of the hard drive controls. The method chosen to do the overwrite as well as serial numbers and asset identifiers should be included in the report. If the overwrite fails for any unaddressable sectors of the hard drive, that should be included in the report as well.

The best practice is to use software tools for overwriting that create a digitally signed (and thus tamper-proof) record of the erasure. An audit will follow a discarded PC from decommissioning all the way through to the end of data sanitization and final disposition.

## 1.10   Ecological and Economic Considerations

Motivation for the proper treatment of data at the end of its useful life also includes two important drivers. Sustainability, ESG, and pollution reduction are ecological considerations. In later chapters we expand on the benefits derived from these approaches as well as how new regulations are driving more interest in data sanitization.

Closely coupled with the ecological drivers are economic benefits of data sanitization.

### 1.10.1   Ecological

Decommissioned devices such as laptops, desktops, servers, and phones create a mandate for proper recycling. If the devices are still functioning, they can be refurbished and resold. If they are not recoverable, they can be disassembled and their parts used for repairs, a common case for high-value phones and laptops. Older devices, especially desktops, tend to end up in a crusher. Those materials that pose the greatest ecological threat are separated and treated with special care. Glass from monitors, especially CRT screens, can be pulverized and sintered or further processed into building materials.

The Responsible Recycling (R2) standard maintained by Sustainable Electronics Recycling International (SERI) is devised to provide auditable procedures for facilities that recycle gear. Those facilities are run by ITAD firms. They have strict procedures for handling equipment to ensure that device provenance is maintained from shipping dock to final destination. Those procedures include data sanitization and record keeping. The ITAD industry has emerged step-by-step since the early 1990s. Today it is a mature global industry with many large and professional companies offering services and solutions. See the stories from executives at three of the largest ITADs in the world in Chapter 9, "Stories from the Field." Each of them has evolved its processes to promote sustainability.

### 1.10.2   Economic

A data sanitization program includes cost savings. First there is the reduced expenditure for storage if old data is systematically erased, removed forever from the cycle of backups and data protection measures.

Data sanitization can be justified by the reduced exposure to regulatory actions, accidental data loss, and legal discovery.

Finally, if data is safely removed from valuable gear such as laptops, servers, and mobile devices, the remaining value in them can be recovered. Many data centers, either private or multiuser colocation centers, have strict policies against data being removed from their facilities. But any facility that has thousands of hard drives for storage is going to experience hard drive failures. High-end hard drives are usually under warranty, but sending hard drives back to the manufacturer is not permitted if they have customer data on them. A hard drive failure means a hard drive is removed and stored in a secure closet while a new one replaces it. A data sanitization program can erase the data on failing hard drives and verify that it has truly been sanitized, allowing the value from returned material allowance (RMA) to be recouped.

## 1.11    Summary: Proactive Risk Reduction and Reactive End of Life

Data sanitization combines technology and processes to ensure that data is properly eradicated at the end of its useful life. A data management program will ensure that only required data is collected in the first place, avoiding further controls that would have to be put in place to be compliant with data privacy regulations. Data sanitization completes the lifecycle for data. It was created, collected, stored, used, disseminated, backed up, and finally sanitized. The end of life of data is the moment that resources are no longer expended to protect it from loss, theft, discovery, or a major breach. The last line of cyber defense is drawn around data, and the last time any process is applied to data is the day it is sanitized.

# Where Are We, and How Did We Get Here?

As long as there has been digital data there has been a need to destroy it, if only to make room for fresher data. When data was recorded on punch cards or paper tape, erasure was a simple matter of burning or shredding the medium. One of the most unusual ways to store data in the early days of digital computers was via acoustic storage. A long wire in a metal housing that bore a resemblance to latter-day hard drive cases was coiled on one end and led to a read-write "head" at the other. Writing involved a timed hammer that would strike the wire creating an acoustic impulse that would travel along the wire in its many coils. When this acoustic wave returned from its journey around the coil, a pickup would "read" it and cause the hammer to re-strike the wire in the same time slot as the original. This would create a record of precisely timed acoustic signals traveling around the wire. Erasure was simply a matter of not striking the wire again or cutting power to the storage device.

## 2.1   Digital Data Storage

Digital data storage is simply a matter of recording ones and zeros in a way that can be read. This could be done with beads on a string, with a bead representing a 1 and a gap representing a 0. A byte could be 8, 16, 32, or 64, beads+gaps. Any recorded data could be erased by simply shoving all the beads to one end of the string, leaving a "message" that was all ones followed by all zeros. Imagine making the beads smaller and smaller and the string thinner and thinner until you store a million bytes in this way. You would need something to read the beads and gaps, perhaps a lightweight lever as sensitive as a phonograph needle that would flip a switch when it encountered a bead. You could have another mechanism to shove the beads into position to record. The read-write levers could travel up and down the string recording and retrieving patterns of ones and zeros.

Mechanical systems, be they patterns punched into paper, beads on a string, or acoustic waves, were soon displaced by much faster digital recording devices. A magnetic head would pass over a metal-coated surface and magnetize a fuzzy but discernible spot on a magnetic tape, streaming by the recording head. Or in the case of hard drives, the recording head would swing over a metallicized spinning platter.

The first disk drive was produced by IBM in 1956. The IBM 350 could store 3.75 megabytes on its 52 platters, each 24 inches in diameter. Disk drives in the '60s and '70s resembled washing machines in size.

There were removable stacks of platters that could be swapped out. Removable media had its own evolution from these canisters to thin plastic disks encased in stiff paper with a read-write window in them. As technology advanced, storage on these "floppy disks" became denser and denser, and the form factor shrunk, from 10" to 3 1/4". There were even mini floppy disks for some game systems.

Magnetic tapes also increased their storage density as they evolved from reel-to-reel tapes to cartridges. Eventually cartridge tapes would be stacked in vast silos, and robotic arms would retrieve the correct one when it was called for and insert it in the read-write system like an eight-track cartridge in a car stereo.

To understand data erasure, you have to understand formatting of magnetic media. Tapes are one thing; they are linear. Disks consist of many concentric rings of tracks. Either way, the magnetic medium is formatted with blocks that are assigned addresses.

Digital data is stored in blocks. The computer preparing a file for storage breaks the file into suitably sized chunks and assigns each chunk to a preformatted area on the tape or disk. With tapes this is done sequentially to reduce the seek time to retrieve the file when it is needed. Disks are more versatile. They spin constantly at a fixed speed as the read-write head traverses the surface radially. The blocks can be written willy-nilly as long as the computer keeps track of where each block is recorded. A disk drive usually has multiple platters and read-write heads on a single arm that swings between the platters. Density of data storage has followed its own Moore's law. Today's disk drives contain terabytes of data.

## 2.2 Erasing Magnetic Media

For the moment imagine taking the Encyclopedia Britannica and storing each word in a different place on a hard drive. A ledger would tell you how to retrieve the words in the correct order to assemble them into readable articles. Destroy the ledger and you would not be able to derive any more value from the stored media than you would an unalphabetized list of all the words in the English language (with many repetitions). This is what happens when you ask an operating system to "erase" a file or move it to the "trash bin." The record of pointers to the storage blocks is simply removed. All the data is still there; it is just impossible for the operating system to retrieve and reassemble them. You would need a forensic tool, which can read each sector on a disk, to display all the data. It would be a puzzle to figure out but not impossible. Imagine the "erased" file was a list of names and credit cards. It would be easy to retrieve them.

When a file is "erased" by an operating system, the blocks it was assigned to are identified as free space, ready to be overwritten with the next file to be saved. Free space in a storage medium can provide a rich hunting ground for law enforcement or cybercriminals looking for pay dirt. But in a working hard drive, it has a half-life. As the system is used, the free space is eventually overwritten with new data. This leads to the idea of true data erasure, or wiping. When the instruction to wipe a file is received, the operating system is told to overwrite the space occupied by the file. This could be simply "overwrite the blocks with all zeros or all ones," or it could be a more complicated algorithm to overwrite the space with a series of passes that could be a combination of random passes, all ones, all zeros, or some other pattern.

In the next chapter, we will cover why more sophisticated patterns of ones and zeros are used, but for the purposes of this discussion, once data is overwritten, it is not recoverable by the forensic tools already mentioned.

## 2.3 History of Data Erasure

We now have enough of an understanding of data storage to relate the history of data erasure.

The world of spy versus spy is replete with stories of data destruction. Much like encoded messages with early forms of encryption dating back to before Caesar's time, data destruction predates digital storage. A secret instruction to an operative behind enemy lines would have to be destroyed after it was received. Instructions from the British Admiralty to a ship captain would be tied to a lead weight and tossed overboard before he would surrender his ship. Written messages would be burned and the ashes stirred when a command post was on the verge of being captured. Or a spy would masticate and swallow a decoded message to ensure it never fell into enemy hands.

One of the authors was in Taiwan speaking about data erasure when he was invited to dinner with a small group of people who wanted to show off a local hero, introduced as the "Steve Jobs of Taiwan." He earned his entrepreneurial reputation when he submitted a proposal to the U.S. Navy for destruction of nuclear launch codes back when they were written on foil encased in a thin breakable container.

You've seen the movies. The President orders a missile launch from a submarine. The captain opens a safe and retrieves the thin case containing the foil and breaks it open revealing the super-secret code. The codes were generated using some system or algorithm that may be subject to deciphering if an enemy ever got hold of them. When a submarine returned to base after its six month stint under the surface, those launch codes would be replaced with new ones. What to do with the now unusable old codes to prevent them from ever falling into the wrong hands?

The Taiwanese Steve Jobs recounted how he went to a local homeware store and wandered the aisles for ideas. He saw a common kitchen implement that every household in Taiwan owns: a small ceramic bowl with a lid and holes for ventilation. He proposed to the Navy that he could supply these for several thousand dollars to the Navy for burning the slips of foil safely on a submarine, and he won the contract. He earned over a thousand times return on his cost of goods sold. As the Cold War progressed, the Navy modernized and eventually distributed nuclear launch codes on CDs. How to destroy these? Our entrepreneur returned to the same store and took the same walk up and down the aisles. He settled on a home ice shaver used to make snow cones. Instead of the frozen cylinder of ice being scraped by a blade, the CD could be inserted, and the layer of data could be scraped from the CD, rendering it unreadable. He sold these devices for even more money.

The story of how to destroy nuclear launch codes after they are replaced involves the best example of data that is at the top of the Top Secret pyramid. In the commercial world, the secret formula for Coke is the best example of "crown jewel" data. All data has value, at least when it is created, but some data has more value than other data. Often, the negative value associated with that data being lost or stolen is even greater. Hospital medical records is one such category. While a patient's vital signs may have negligible value a short time after they are recorded, the loss of that data could lead to a HIPAA violation and tens of thousands of dollars in fines.

## 2.3.1    The Beginnings of Commercial Data Erasure

In the early 1990s Kim Väisänen and Janne Tervo started a business called Karelian Innovations to control engine block heaters in cars parked in garages. They lived in Joensuu, Finland, where winters are long and engine block heaters are common. They used data-over-power lines to send signals to the heaters to turn them on and off. It worked great in the countryside where power was relatively clean but did not work well in urban environments, which were noisier. A microwave oven in a house could completely garble any attempt to use data-over-power lines. The business did not succeed, and Kim and his partner moved on.

At that time in Finland there was a vibrant after market for used computers. The local hospital was selling its old computers, often to neighboring Russia. Kim's partner, Janne, purchased one of those computers and discovered records of 40,000 patients stored on it. Kim's good friend was a journalist for the largest paper in Scandinavia. They gave him the story, and he wrote one of the first data breach stories about the incident.

That incident got Kim and Janne thinking about how to solve the problem of data residing on used or discarded hard drives, and they came up with their next venture. Blancco Oy was launched in 1998 and shipped its first data erasure program on floppy disks in 1999.

Kim relates that there was a Norwegian company that went public during the dot-com boom that had a competing data erasure product. Norman Ibas was in the data recovery business primarily. Eventually they lost ground to Blancco and ended up negotiating a deal with Blancco to hand over their data erasure business to them.

Blancco was sold to a private equity company in 2014, which took it public on the London Stock Exchange.

White Canyon started shipping its WipeDrive product in 1996. It eventually changed the company name to WipeDrive and was acquired by Blancco in 2022.

## 2.3.2    Darik's Boot and Nuke (DBAN)

Darik Horn got into technology as a teenager. In 1993 he wanted access to the Internet but could not afford the long-distance charges to Toronto. So, he helped build one of the first Internet service providers (ISPs) in southwestern Ontario. He relates being exposed to data security and encryption when his manager gave him a copy of Bruce Schneier's seminal book, *Applied Cryptography* (Wiley, 1995). He enrolled at the University of Waterloo, well known for its encryption program, to earn a degree in mathematics. In the early 2000s, while still in the undergraduate program, he was working nights and weekends as an IT manager for a logistics software company. Their customers kept business-critical data in the company's IT infrastructure.

Late one night, his employer texted him to say that he should go home because the company was bankrupt and had closed that morning. As he tells the story, Horn didn't have anything better to do, so he kept coming to work to keep the servers running and help people migrate off their platform.

> "Somebody told me that all corporate property was going to public auction and asked if the servers contained anything valuable. This conversation got me thinking about what I could do to protect our users before they got unplugged. I couldn't find anything that fit, so I created DBAN, and the first person to ever see it running was a bailiff sent by the liquidating trustee."
>
> *From an email from Darik Horn*

When he left that company, Horn published DBAN to SourceForge, June 10, 2002, and forgot about it. A year or two later he was asked about DBAN in a job interview but didn't know what they were talking about. He went back to SourceForge, saw the download statistics and several bug reports, and figured that he should properly maintain the software because people were using it.

During the 2000s, the regulatory environment changed such that certain organizations couldn't dispose of computer equipment without a data destruction process. "Nobody knew how to do this, and DBAN was usually the first solution that they found. I became a subject-matter expert if only because I was getting desperate cold calls," he said.

Electronics recyclers that couldn't do data destruction were being forced out of the computer segment, one of the few profitable areas. DBAN found a revenue niche here because it was lower cost than the market leader of the day.

Horn quit graduate school and worked progressively fewer hours at his day job as his income from consulting on DBAN increased.

Development and support of DBAN was acquired by an ITAD named Global Electric Electronic Processing (GEEP) in 2009. Blancco Technology Group acquired DBAN from GEEP in 2012 and makes it available today at dban.org. It is still downloaded thousands of times a month for personal use. It must be pointed out that DBAN is a generic tool that is probably adequate for home or hobbyist use to wipe most data from a laptop. The user has to have some level of computer savvy to download an image to a thumb drive and then boot the target machine from that thumb drive to initiate the erasure process. If they are selling the computer or passing it on to a friend or relative, they will have to reinstall the desired OS and applications to make it useful. This process can take many hours, first to erase and then to install the OS.

Webroot Software (now part of OpenText) produced a product called Window Washer that could target individual files for overwriting. It was discontinued in 2005 when Webroot changed its direction to focus on its SpySweeper product.

SecureIT was a Swedish startup that developed file erasure technology. It too was acquired by Blancco. (Fredrik Forslund was one of the founders.)

## 2.4  Summary

Data sanitization solutions continue to evolve as technology changes. Mobile device management (MDM) solutions can be configured to wipe data if a phone is reported lost or stolen or if an employee leaves an organization. Often the corporate data resides in a container that is owned and controlled by the employer, so they have the right to wipe it. Cloud storage presents a unique challenge because there are so many places data can reside, from Kubernetes configurations that are updated continuously to snapshot images of complete VMs.

As new forms of data storage are developed, new means of data sanitization have to follow. Expanding regulations are driving the requirement that new devices be repairable and reusable. ITADs, hyperscalers, enterprises, and large data center operators will have to accommodate these regulations as they plan their data storage requirements. Chapter 15, "The Future of Data Sanitization" addresses some of the directions that data storage could take from doped quartz to DNA (easily the highest data density) to quantum storage.

# Data Sanitization Technology

There are as many ways to destroy data as there are to store it. All data should be accounted for in a plan of data lifecycle management. Paper records should be stored and accessible for easy retrieval in case a legal discovery process is kicked off. But after their useful and legal life, they should be destroyed in an ecologically sound way. This means shredding and recycling. For most purposes, a simple longitudinal shredding process is sufficient. The effort to reassemble 4 mm strips of paper into their original form is too expensive for all but the most critical records. That effort is insurmountable if the shredding process mixes the documents with large quantities of other documents. Scanning the strips and puzzling out the original content is however possible. Cross-cut shredders are the best practice today. Even then, the shredded documents should be protected until they can be pulped.

Physical destruction of digital storage media has similar requirements. The ecological factors are much greater with PCs, hard drives, thumb drives, and SIM cards. The following processes are required for R2 certification. It is surprisingly common for people to drill a hole through a hard drive to render it inoperable, which it certainly does. But only the data at the drill site is actually destroyed. The rest of the data is recoverable in a forensics lab.

## 3.1   Shredding

Storage device shredders physically mangle and chop the entire device into pieces that must be less than 20 mm square. The storage device must be removed from the computer or array it is part of and thoroughly documented. Asset numbers, serial numbers, and the machine it came from must be recorded to create an auditable record of destruction. Often, photographs of the identifiers are recorded. The point is to be able to provide the assurance that a particular drive associated with a particular machine can be shown to have been destroyed and the data that may have been on the machine be irrecoverable.

Specialized shredders are employed to destroy SIM cards and SD memory cards that can contain up to 2 terabytes of data. The R2 requirement is to pulverize these memory devices to pieces smaller than 4 mm on a side. At the density of modern solid-state storage, even a shard of 16 square mm will have recoverable data on it, but the processes for extracting such data have not been demonstrated in open source literature. As always, it is assumed that if an extraction technique is theoretically possible, various national intelligence agencies are capable of it.

Solid-state drives (SSDs) should be treated like SIM and SD cards and similarly pulverized. This may require removing the silicon chips from the boards they are on.

## 3.2   Degaussing

Anyone who remembers laying a 3 ¼" floppy disk on a magnet will be familiar with this manner of destroying recorded data. Because the physical bits are microscopic areas of a tape or hard disk platter that have been magnetized, exposing the medium to a strong magnetic field will erase all the data.

Commercial degaussers are the size of a small refrigerator. A loose drive, 9" tape, or an entire laptop can be put inside, and a strong electromagnet is activated to expose the media to a magnetic field that effectively messes up all the magnetized bits. Boot sectors and everything are erased. Even delicate hardware components could be destroyed. Thus, degaussing is considered physical destruction and is not used for devices meant to be refurbished or reused in any way.

You must use caution around a degausser. Any storage media within range could be damaged. They should be placed in a separate area and warnings posted, especially to those wearing medical devices like pacemakers.

Degaussing of some media, like audio tapes and floppy disks, may leave them reusable. But hard drives have servo-control tracks written to the platters by the manufacturers. These tracks allow the read-write head to find its place over a track even if the hard drive is subjected to an impact or it changes size with temperature. If those servo-control tracks are destroyed in a degausser, the hard drive is no longer usable.

Note that degaussing is not an option for SSD memory. Pulverizing, incinerating, or melting are effective, although not the most environmentally responsible methods.

Organizations that handle highly sensitive material, such as an intelligence agency, will specify degaussing followed by physical shredding for any magnetic media. Most other organizations consider one method to be sufficient. That said, because the disk sectors and all formatting are gone, it is not possible to verify that the data is not there after a device has been degaussed. Recall the hot and cold spots in the dinner you are reheating in your microwave oven. A "cold spot" in a degausser may leave data intact.

## 3.3   Overwriting

Most of the field of data sanitization is concerned with effective means of overwriting storage media without physically destroying the device. Various schemes for doing so have been around for decades. They include the following:

**Single-Pass Overwriting**   For magnetic media, simply overwrite the file or entire disk with the following:

- All ones
- All zeros
- A random sequence of ones and zeros

After a single pass, it is theorized that laboratory tools could be used to decipher the original magnetic state of each bit on the platter or tape. Indeed, the original work by Peter Gutman published in 1996 described how this is done at least against the storage densities on hard drives at the time.

It is ironic that at a microscopic scale digital data is actually recorded in an analog manner in fuzzy magnetic domains. Along the individual tracks of a hard drive platter, measuring only a few microns in width, the write head magnetizes a portion of the track to represent a single bit. Gutman showed that by positioning a very small magnetic probe on a cantilever arm and then measuring the probe's displacement, it was possible to discern the previous state of the bit and theoretically, thanks to the small positional variances each time the write head passed over the disk, all of the previous states.

When a disk drive only contained 20 MB of data, the area required to record a magnetic state representing a one or zero was much larger than in a 6 TB disk today. In other words, a tool such as a scanning electron microscope or a sensitive probe could discern what the state of the particular molecules was before being overwritten.

This theoretical fear that data can be recovered from magnetic media has given rise to much more stringent standards required by intelligence and military agencies around the world.

The next level of assurance for complete data erasure is to overwrite three times with some sequence involving a random pass, all ones, and then all zeros. This has become the default guidance for the U.S. military.

**Gutman Method of 35 Passes**    Peter Gutman determined in 1996 that ensuring that all possible combinations of timing bits and data bits were overwritten in such a way as to defeat the analysis techniques would require 35 passes. Unfortunately, the time required to completely overwrite every sector of a large hard drive 35 times could be several days. Even Gutman has updated his original paper from 1996 to say that a single pass of a modern hard drive is sufficient. Besides, that much writing would probably wear out the mechanical components of a hard drive and diminish its useful life significantly. One data destruction company in Mexico was asked to use this spec on an entire data center. Luckily, cooler heads prevailed.

**Bruce Schneier**    Cryptography expert Bruce Schneier devised his own overwrite standard in 1996. He specifies a pass of all ones followed by a pass of all ones and then seven passes with randomized bits.

**The DoD 5220.22-M**    This standard was first published in 1995. It originally called for three passes (all ones, all zeros, and a random pass). It has gone through several revisions with one version calling for seven overwrite passes. But today the Department of Defense either recommends NIST 800-88 or the Defense Security Service (DSS) publication Clearing and Sanitization Matrix (C&SM).

DSS, the DoD agency that administers and implements the defense portion of the National Industrial Security Program (NISP), including the NISPOM, updated its "Assessment and Authorization Process Manual (DAAPM)" for federal contractors effective May 6, 2019. The media sanitization guidelines portion in that document specifies NIST SP 800-88 as a primary guideline for media sanitization (pp 46, 130-31).

**NIST Special Publication 800-88**    This calls for a single-pass overwrite.

## 3.4    Crypto-Erase

If you are looking to randomize the data on a hard drive or SSD, look no further than encrypted data. To all but the holder of the decryption key, the data is essentially random. A victim of ransomware will attest to this.

If full disk encryption is used on a laptop, storage array, or cell phone, then you don't actually have to overwrite storage. You just have to destroy the encryption keys. This is much faster than overwriting and is used for erasing most mobile phones today. But, the devil is in the details. Have you found all copies of the keys? Sometimes recovery keys are stored somewhere else. Recovery keys for Microsoft's full disk encryption (FDE) tool, called BitLocker, are stored in Active Directory. If a user or administrator suspends BitLocker on an endpoint, the recovery key is written to the device's disk in cleartext!

Many other problems have arisen over the years with self-encrypting drives that, in theory, have hardware components that encrypt everything written to disk. The following is from the International Data Sanitization Consortium:

> **"A major issue with FDE is that often the data is not encrypted at all. This has occurred with several self-encrypting drives. A manufacturer defect can mean that the onboard encryption modules are not even turned on by default. Another issue with self-encrypting drives is that the encryption keys may be discoverable through various side-channel attacks which would make the encryption essentially useless."**

A second issue with FDE is key management. The encryption keys may be stored in memory where an attacker can discover them and use them to decrypt the drive. Or, in the case of Microsoft BitLocker, recovery keys may be inadequately protected. While encryption keys are normally protected by the trusted platform module (TPM), in most Windows environments, recovery keys are stored in Active Directory in cleartext. A determined hacker could get access to Active Directory and thus all the recovery keys for all the systems, even those that have been scheduled for recycling or those lost or stolen.

There's one final issue with encryption as a replacement for data sanitization: attacks against encryption algorithms are ongoing. At the least, encryption that is considered infeasible to crack today will be trivial to crack in the future. The MITRE report "Security Requirements For Cryptographic Modules, Information Technology Laboratory, National Institute of Standards and Technology, 2001," states, "Even high-profile algorithms by accomplished cryptographic experts" have been defeated in the past and that "as cryptography advances so rapidly, it is common for an algorithm to be considered 'unsafe' even if it was once thought to be strong."

So, relying completely on encryption has to be considered as a temporal defense. Only complete data sanitization, even of encrypted data, which implies testing to ensure that destruction has taken place, serves to ensure that data from lost, stolen, or recycled equipment will never come back to haunt you.

For your encrypted hard drives, look to these four steps to ensure data sanitization:

1. Test to make sure the drives are actually encrypting data when first put into production.

2. When disposing of these devices, find and securely overwrite all keys.

3. Test media to ensure that all sectors are indeed encrypted.

4. Create a tamper-proof audit report.

Modern smartphones have the ability to encrypt everything with iPhones set to encrypt by default. Simply overwriting the keys or choosing a factory reset will make all the data unavailable. Yet, if the phone has network access, it may actually resync with a cloud backup service and restore all the keys. So, handling of data sanitization in a refurbishing facility has to be carefully orchestrated to prevent that from happening after key destruction.

## 3.5    Erasing Solid-State Drives

The era of spinning platters for data storage is coming to an end. As solid-state drives increase in capacity while dropping in cost, the worldwide volume for SSDs is expected to have surpassed HDDs in 2021.

Storing data in silicon is dramatically different than magnetic media storage. On a hard drive, a bit is a microscopic area that is magnetically polarized. It is subject to degaussing and overwriting to wipe data. Silicon wafers, on the other hand, are etched with circuitry that creates gates. Each gate holds a state that is dependent on electric charge, not the orientation of magnetic dipoles.

These solid-state storage devices also have computing capability to direct which data is stored in which memory location. The instruction sets programmed into the chips, be they cell phone SIM cards, memory chips on a desktop or server, or full-fledged SSDs, control location, and basic functions, like erasing.

SSDs have different physical characteristics from HDDs. Like hard drives, solid-state drives can develop bad memory locations. The controller has to keep track of those locations and skip over them. Because they rely on electrical charge, SSDs have a tendency to wear out. Individual bits can take only so many cycles of charging. Thus, the controller is designed to distribute stored data to even out the amount of wear on individual bits.

While memory chips are subject to forensic attack, they are inherently better than hard disks. Flipping a bit in silicon does not leave a ghost image behind of its previous state. Forensics focuses on bypassing controls in the chip logic and gaining direct access to the bits. Even more sophisticated forensic attacks involve removing the protective casing of a memory chip to expose the underlying microscopic circuitry and then attempting to observe the state of the individual bits. Other means have been demonstrated in laboratory experiments to attack solid-state devices; they are usually destructive and can involve heating, etching, and even putting the device in a microwave oven.

Erasing data from solid-state memory is, by design, simple. The control language for most solid-state storage contains a command for resetting each bit in a memory location to an initial state, effectively erasing the data. But there are cases of those commands not actually working. How can you know that just because you told the operating system to erase a file that the file management system issued the correct command to the memory device and that the memory device executed the command? A bug anywhere in the path could cause data erasure to fail.

Like other storage media, solid-state devices have to be sanitized before physical ownership of the device is relinquished. Large SSDs from a data center, USB thumb drives or SSDs, SIM cards, and wearables are all devices that should undergo data sanitization before they are either refurbished for resale or discarded. The process is similar, but the technology is different. Instead of overwriting, a command is issued to the memory controller. A forensic pass to verify that all the sectors have been reset effectively is required.

## 3.6  Bad Blocks

Because every memory location in a NAND chip has a limited life, wear leveling is employed to extend the life of the memory chip. Data is prioritized to those blocks that have the fewest Program/Erase (P/E) counts. Memory locations on a solid-state device may be unreachable by the flash memory controller. In other words, there may be sectors on the device that contain critical data that an attacker may retrieve. If a forensic scan reveals too many of these sectors, the device should be further processed by pulverizing the memory chips. While the R2 standard for hard drives is to shred to pieces that measure less than 20×20 mm, the standard for solid-state memory is 2×2 mm and to deposit the pulverized pieces in a bin with other pulverized chips. The concept is that it may be possible to retrieve data from a single fragment, but finding the piece with the secret nuclear launch code on it would be prohibitively expensive if it were buried in a 55 gallon drum with billions of other pieces.

## 3.7  Data Forensics

Forensics is the practical discovery of information after it has been erased or otherwise hidden. In its broadest meaning, it can include all of the things an investigator may do to piece together evidence to tell a story. You see forensics experts at work in criminal cases examining tire tracks, strands of fabric, blood samples, rifling of a spent rifle round, fingerprints, and DNA. In the data realm, forensics is concerned with finding data and documenting its origin, location, and ownership. Forensic accountants piece together what happened in financial schemes to defraud. Paleo forensics experts examine human remains to determine cause of death. They use dental records and bone records to identify people who are long deceased.

The field of data forensics is broad. A forensics expert may be called on for tasks as varied as follows:

- Discover violations of corporate policy like an employee using corporate resources to engage in illegal activities. This may involve examining the employee's browsing history for evidence that they were visiting inappropriate websites.

- Discover evidence of tampering by looking for the absence of log data.

- Post-mortem of a breach. Part of an incident response activity is to determine what happened. The forensics team attempts to determine the exact time of compromise and how it was accomplished and then track the progress of the attacker as they make their way from machine to machine to get to the data or target they are after.

- Reconstruct a file after it has been lost. This could be a file that somebody "erased" but did not sanitize. It could be to recover a valuable file from a hard drive with corrupted sectors that made the file unreadable. Or perhaps the hard drive itself failed, but the data is intact.

- Some of the most valuable information in the world is in the form of crypto currencies.

A data forensics expert may be called on to recover Bitcoin from a hard drive or solid-state wallet.

You can see that data forensics is the field of anti-sanitization. It is what is being referred to when a NIST or other standard calls for making data "unrecoverable using laboratory techniques."

Forensics used to be a proportionally larger component of the field of cybersecurity. It has not shrunk; it has just been overshadowed by so many new security requirements (firewalls, endpoint protection, threat intelligence). Extracting data from loose hard drives, computers, and cell phones is still the daily task of crime investigators.

Even the military makes use of forensics for counter insurgency. After an insurgent cell is captured, the forensics experts get to work. They grab data off of phones to determine where the next level of command was when they were receiving instructions. They then target that new team.

At one point, the chief of police of NYPD stated that every crime is cyber-crime, meaning that cell phones and the data on them were the primary investigative tool.

Forensics investigations have to be carefully handled to produce admissible evidence in court. Typically a hard drive or phone of interest is cloned so that the original evidence is not disturbed. Only then is the cloned hard drive examined for deleted files and other evidence.

EnCase Forensic is the standard for professional investigations. It was created by Guidance Software in 1998. Guidance was acquired by OpenText in 2017. EnCase is a bundle of tools for discovering and recording data from many different devices. A portable forensics lab can include EnCase running on a laptop with dozens of connectors for all the different types of hard drives and phones. EnCase is also a case management platform to handle and make sense of all the disparate pieces of evidence collected.

Forensic tools like EnCase and many open source solutions use native capabilities of an operating system to directly access storage media. Instead of looking at the OS directory and file system, it can read sectors directly from a hard drive. It can then piece together files from sectors scattered all over the device.

Often investigators are interested in so-called free space. These are areas on the media that potentially contain data that has been deleted. A suspect may have thought they were destroying incriminating evidence when they emptied their trash bin, but it is still there for a forensics analyst to uncover.

Note that while NIST and other standards bodies refer to laboratory techniques for extracting data from storage media, they usually mean using forensic tools such as the ones described. The techniques for using sensitive instruments to read the ghosts of previously written data are rarely employed. That's not to say that intelligence agencies don't use these techniques.

Modern data sanitization software not only overwrites free space along with all the sectors on a storage device, but they sample the sectors afterward to test for success. In essence, they perform a forensic sampling of the data. The tools can look for confirmation that the sectors have been overwritten with the designated pattern of zeros and ones or test for the randomness exhibited by encrypted data if the device were crypto-erased.

## 3.8  Summary

In this chapter, we explored all the means of destroying data from physical destruction to software for overwriting. We wrapped up with a discussion of the wide field of data forensics, which seeks to overcome attempts to sanitize data and plays an important role in the verification of data erasure, a required step in the data sanitization process. In the next chapter, we look at information lifecycle management, the formal process from tracking data from creation to its end of life.

# Information Lifecycle Management

## 4.1   Information Lifecycle Management vs. Data Lifecycle Management

Data lifecycle management (DLM) is the term applied to a program that tracks attributes of files such as age, creation date, size, format, and other metadata. DLM programs are supported by commercial products mostly concerned with tracking where each file is stored and how long it should be kept available for access before it is archived. Backup and recovery plans can be developed from

DLM programs. The term DLM is often used interchangeably with *information lifecycle management* (ILM). There is an important distinction. ILM goes beyond these general attributes to search for various types of data that might appear within those files, such as national identity numbers, credit card numbers, and other personal information.

Again, the distinction between ILM and DLM is important. The EU General Data Protection Regulation, for instance, defines the right to erasure in Article 17, often called the right to be forgotten. Data subjects are given the right to request their information to be erased upon request—with proof that the information has truly been "forgotten." Locating a customer's data in files, databases, and even backups is required to comply with privacy regulations. Beyond the regulatory needs, being able to track particular data types throughout their lifecycle is critical for security and legal discovery processes.

## 4.2 Information Lifecycle Management

ILM is a comprehensive approach to managing the flow of an information system's data and associated metadata from creation and initial storage to the time when it becomes obsolete and is destroyed. An important concept to grasp is that all information has a life span that should be tracked until it is put to rest via data sanitization techniques. Even then, a record of its destruction should be kept for an additional length of time (yes, records of data sanitization have their own lifecycle).

### 4.2.1 Lifecycle Stages

When putting a program in place, the following lifecycle stages are recognized:

**Create** New digital data is generated, or the existing data is modified, which includes any content element—not just a document or database. Data is being created constantly as employees work on documents; machines generate data from their automated processes; financial systems are updated with purchase orders, invoices, and transactions; and sensors on the plant floor record temperatures, counts, and measurements. Practically every automated process creates a log entry. IT security systems generate data at an astounding rate as alerts and logs. A vulnerability scan of all IT assets can create millions of data points. An attacker probing network defenses can generate hundreds of alerts per incident. Network traffic flows can generate terabytes of data; full packet captures even more. In short, data is being created every second of the day.

**Store** Upon creation, most data is immediately committed to a storage system. It is moved from machine memory to a local hard drive, a network-attached storage (NAS), a cloud bucket, or a remote data center. Those storage systems are usually configured as a RAID array to ensure the data is available and uncorrupted. In addition, those storage arrays are backed up on a continuous (mirrored) or scheduled basis, creating multiple copies of every dataset.

**Use**   While data is in use, it is drawn on for computing, manipulation, analysis, or served up for viewing. Unless you are living in a cabin on Walden Pond, you interact with data every day. You check the time when you first awake, answer emails, compose a blog post, make a flight reservation, watch a YouTube training video, or binge-watch Netflix. Your wearable is recording your heart rate and steps walked, and you check it throughout the day directly from your wrist or on the cloud.

**Share**   As data is shared, it is duplicated. Email a slide deck to the team working on a presentation; now everybody has a copy on their local hard drive. Drop a document into a cloud sharing platform, and others can download it to work on it. Multiple versions of this manuscript are being saved in Google Docs even as this sentence is being written. The editors and layout designers will have copies of the final manuscript. The printer will have images of the data to etch into aluminum plates for offset production. Thousands of copies will be distributed as ebooks. The 148 KB file could eventually use more than a terabyte of data storage in all of its formats and replications.

**Archive**   Archiving is different than backing up. The data leaves the "active" state and migrates to long-term storage systems for retention. It could be to tape or even written to CDs. Data management implies that a record is kept of what data is stored and where, so it can be retrieved if needed. Long-term archiving can require reading the data from its current storage medium when it is reaching its expected useful life and rewriting it to the latest storage medium.

SEC Rule 17a-4 is just one regulation (for dealer brokers) that specifically requires archiving to a medium that is *nonerasable*. CDs and DVDs or other Write Once Read Many (WORM) storage may be required.

**Destroy**   Data sanitization is performed to make the data permanently unrecoverable through physical or logical means. This end of life for data also means the end of any security concern for the data.

## 4.3   Data Security Lifecycle

Rich Mogul, an analyst at Securosis, introduced the idea of a data security lifecycle (DSL). While ILS management is an operational and compliance concern, DLS is concerned with protecting the data through the six stages of its life, from creation to destruction. Although it is shown as a linear progression, once created, data can bounce between phases without restriction and may not pass through all stages.

### 4.3.1    Stages for Data Security Lifecycle

These are the stages in detail:

**Create**    Classify the information and determine appropriate rights, usually performed by technology or default classification and rights applied based on identity, device, or geolocation. An example of assigning classifications automatically would be: any spreadsheet created by the finance department gets a higher classification score than one created by the receptionist. Another example may be that access logs to a database are critical. Classification is one of the hardest parts of DSL (just as it is for asset management). A control based on classification could inhibit the ability to share and collaborate.

**Store**    Map the classification and rights to security controls, including access controls, encryption, and rights management. Include certain database controls like labeling in rights management, not just DRM. Controls at this stage also apply to managing content in storage repositories, such as using content discovery to ensure that data is in approved/appropriate repositories.

**Use**    Include both detective controls like activity monitoring and preventative controls like rights management. Logical controls are typically applied in databases and applications.

**Share**    Include a mix of detective and preventive controls, such as DLP/CMF/CMP and encryption for secure exchange of data, as well as logical controls and application security.

**Archive**    Use a combination of encryption and asset management to protect the data and ensure its availability.

**Destroy**    Use an effective data sanitization method to deliberately, permanently, and irreversibly remove or destroy the data. This process involves going back through the archive, storage, and sharing locations of that data (where the data has been located) to permanently make it unrecoverable.

## 4.4    Data Hygiene

Data hygiene is the process of ensuring all incorrect, duplicate, or unused data is properly classified and migrated into the appropriate lifecycle stage for storage, archival, or destruction on an ongoing basis through automated policy enforcement. By following the best data hygiene practices, organizations are able to effectively manage "where" their data is throughout the lifecycle and reduce the amount of data they store by successfully destroying the data to mitigate risks.

## 4.5 Data Sanitization

Data sanitization is the process of deliberately, permanently, and irreversibly removing or destroying the data stored on a memory device to make it unrecoverable. A device that has been sanitized has no usable residual data, and even with the assistance of advanced forensic tools, the data will never be recovered.

There are three methods to achieve data sanitization: physical destruction, cryptographic erasure, and data erasure.

### 4.5.1 Physical Destruction

Physical destruction is the process of shredding hard drives, smartphones, printers, laptops, and other storage media into tiny pieces by large mechanical shredders or using degaussers.

Degaussing is a form of physical destruction whereby data is exposed to the powerful magnetic field of a degausser and neutralized, rendering the data unrecoverable. Degaussing can be achieved only on hard disk drives (HDDs) and most tapes, but the drives or tapes cannot be reused upon completion. Degaussing is not an effective method of data sanitization on solid-state drives (SSDs).

Physical destruction is an effective method of destroying data to render the data unrecoverable and achieve data sanitization. Physical destruction can be harmful to the environment and destroys the assets so they are unable to be reused or resold.

### 4.5.2 Cryptographic Erasure

Cryptographic erasure is used interchangeably with crypto-erase. Cryptographic erasure is the process of using encryption software (either built-in or deployed) on the entire data storage device and erasing the key used to decrypt the data. The encryption algorithm must be at a minimum of 128 bits. While the data remains on the storage device itself, by erasing the original key, the data is effectively impossible to decrypt. As a result, the data is rendered unrecoverable and is an appropriate method to achieve data sanitization.

Here are three steps to achieve cryptographic erasure:

1. The encryption on the storage device must be turned on by default and provide access to the API call to the storage device to remove the key, which allows cryptographic erasure to be supported.

2. Cryptographic erasure must ensure that the old encryption keys have been removed and replaced with a new key, rendering the data encrypted and the previous key unrecoverable.

3. The cryptographic erasure software must produce a tamper-proof certificate containing information that the key has been successfully removed, along with data about the device and standard used.

Cryptographic erasure is a quick and effective method to achieve data sanitization. It is best used when storage devices are in transit or for storage devices that contain information that is not sensitive. Cryptographic erasure relies heavily on the manufacturer where implementation issues could occur. The users also could impact the success of cryptographic erasure through broken keys and human errors. But most importantly, cryptographic erasure still allows for the data to remain on the storage device and often does not achieve the regulatory compliance requirements.

### 4.5.3  Data Erasure

Data erasure is the software-based method of securely overwriting data from any data storage device, using zeros and ones, onto all sectors of the device. By overwriting the data on the storage device, the data is rendered unrecoverable and achieves data sanitization.

To achieve data erasure, the software must do the following:

■ Allow for selection of a specific standard, based on your industry and organization's unique needs.

■ Verify the overwriting methodology has been successful and has removed data across the entire device, or target data (if specifically called for).

■ Produce a tamper-proof certificate containing information that the erasure has been successful and written to all sectors of the device, along with data about the device and standard used.

Block erase can be a feature but is often used interchangeably with data erasure. Block erase is the ability for vendor software to target the logical block addresses, including those that are not currently mapped to active addresses, on the storage device to erase all data on the device. However, if the block erase software does not provide for the three steps noted in the data erasure definition, it does not achieve data sanitization.

Data sanitization is the highest form of securing data within data erasure, due to the validation process for ensuring the data was successfully overwritten and the auditable reporting readily available. Data erasure also supports environmental initiatives, while allowing organizations to retain the resale value of the storage devices. Data erasure is a more efficient process than other forms of data sanitization. It preserves the device for reuse and does not generate waste in the form of crushed hard drives or powdered SSDs. Data erasure forces organizations to develop policies and processes for all data storage devices.

## 4.6  Summary

It's one thing to understand the different means of destroying data. It's another to implement a repeatable and verifiable process. The following chapter introduces the requirements of various regulatory regimes that have come about since 1995 to ensure that data is protected from loss or theft or even inadvertent exposure. Particular attention is paid to those laws, regulations, and standards that address data sanitization. This book aims to build a case for data sanitization for its inherent benefits in improving security and reducing data management costs. But, as is so often the case, justifying budgets for new processes needs the additional motivation of compliance.

# Regulatory Requirements

Four separate regimes drive the need for data sanitization. The fourth, ESG, is facilitated by data sanitization. Data retention requirements, data privacy regulations, and IT security frameworks all call for data sanitization, whereas ecological and social governance requirements call for reuse of electronic components to reduce waste. Regulations exist to codify requirements often set forth in standards. In this chapter, we introduce the main regulations, frameworks, and standards that touch on data sanitization, data protection, and privacy.

## 5.1    Frameworks

A data security framework is a structured list, almost an outline or a matrix, of measures to be applied to a problem. ISO 25001-2 is such an outline with sections devoted to all aspects of an information security management system. The NIST Cybersecurity Framework is built around Identify, Protect, Detect, Respond, Recover. Frameworks dictate the use of controls, but they do not prescribe the controls. ISO is almost wholly about maintaining a security information management system but does not specify the types of technology used for the SIMs (subscriber identity modules).

The following are the major frameworks and how they can be interpreted to apply to data sanitization measures:

- **ISO 27001** crosses the boundary between a standard and a framework. It is a general framework for Information Security Management Systems. Being certified by an approved auditor means that an organization has documented processes that it follows to ensure the proper handling of information and the ability to respond to breach and other incidents. ISO 27002 provides detailed controls to accompany 207001.

- **Information Technology Infrastructure Library** (ITIL) was originally a general framework for IT service management. In 2019 ITIL v4 changed the focus to general service management.

- **Control Objectives for Information and Related Technologies (COBIT)** was created by ISACA to provide a general framework for the management and governance of IT systems.

### 5.1.1    NIST Cybersecurity Framework Applied to Data

The following components of a data security and compliance framework are aligned with the NIST Cybersecurity Framework. A consistent framework applied across data repositories will provide protection.

Identify    Identify the types of data and the data repositories that hold them. Do so even in a dynamic environment where datasets are duplicated, backed up, restored, and deleted often. Map the network locations of the data and the network control points. This discovery and classification of data (and the databases that hold the data) is specifically called for by both GDPR and CPRA. An extension of Demming's "You can't control what you can't measure" would be "You cannot measure what you cannot see."

**Protect**   Protect the data from improper data creation, reads, updates, and deletions (CRUD). In SQL, for instance, the Data Definition Language (DDL) defines rules for CREATE, ALTER, and DROP actions. Apply a least privilege access policy. Require strong authentication for critical operations. Enforce network connectivity policies.

**Detect**   Detect when policies are bypassed or attempts are made to bypass policy that could indicate an attack. Monitor and alert on unusual behavior. Protections invariably serve as mere speed bumps to an attacker who seeks to gain access to an account with privileged access or exploit a zero-day vulnerability to gain access. Detection and alerting are backstops to protection.

**Respond**   Have a documented process in place to respond to improper data access. Answer the questions: Which roles are responsible for the response? What authorities do they have to act? What reports should be generated? Who should be notified (internal audit, executives, regulatory body, or law enforcement)? Use automated tools to react to detected breaches in a timely manner. According to the Ponemon Institute, the average time between a breach and discovery is 206 days, while the average time to contain a breach is 73 days. Shorten the detection time and use automated tools to triage what happened and what controls need to be put in place to prevent a recurrence.

**Recover**   Recover lost or compromised data. Restore the database to a trusted good state. Apply additional controls to avoid a repetition of the incident. Recall the Office of Personnel Management (OPM), which recognized multiple attacks and breaches of its databases. It had put in a budget request for funds to build up its security. In the meantime, a group of state hackers breached and exfiltrated the entire database of records of everyone who had ever applied for a security clearance.

## 5.2   Regulations

Regulations will often refer to the general principles in frameworks, if only as examples of the measures to be put in place. They will also cite explicit standards as developed by standards bodies such as ISO, ANSI, or BSI. Often, laws are created that require adherence to a standard. Because the standards can be updated frequently, the laws do not have to be. In this way, standards can keep up with changes to technologies, and new developments in the IT ecosystem and lawmakers do not have to revisit their requirements. If a law calls for adherence to a standard, the standard becomes the measure that an auditor or regulator will use to determine compliance.

## 5.2.1   GDPR

In 2011 an Austrian law student, Maximillian Schrems, was studying at Santa Clara University in California. He attended a guest lecture by Facebook's privacy lawyer, Ed Palmieri. He was surprised at Palmieri's apparent lack of understanding of the EU's privacy regulations. He made that the subject of his term paper that semester. Then he filed a request to Facebook, under the EU Data Protection Directive, for all the data it had collected on him. He was amazed when he received a CD with 1,222 PDF pages of information, including all of his posts, likes, interactions with advertisers, and even his "pokes" (remember those?). (See the *Right to Erasure in EU Data Protection Law* by Jeff Ausloos for extensive EU case law on erasure.)

Schrems then filed 16 complaints against Facebook's Irish subsidiary with the Irish Data Protection Commissioner (IDPC). Later, in 2013, after the revelations from Edward Snowden, Schrems sought to bar Facebook from exporting data from Ireland to the United States, based on allegations that Facebook shared all of its data with the NSA through the PRISM program.

Ireland punted to the European Court of Justice (CJEU) saying that EU law superseded its own laws. The European Commission had previously (2000) determined that U.S. Safe Harbor laws complied with various EU privacy protection rules. By 2015 the Court of Justice had ruled that the Safe Harbor provisions did not provide adequate protection of privacy.

Schrems continued to press his case as EU regulations and court decisions evolved to support them. In 2018, he filed complaints against Google and Facebook claiming €3.9 billion in fines. He created a nonprofit called None of Your Business (NYOB) to pursue his campaign, which is still ongoing, now that GDPR is in effect and can impose fines up to 4 percent of *revenue* of an offending party. You can imagine how large 4 percent of Google's or Facebook's revenue could be. Alphabet, Google's parent, had $257 billion in revenue in 2021. Meta, Facebook's parent, had $118 billion.

The EU General Data Protection Regulation went into effect May 25, 2018. While supplementing the privacy regulations of member countries, it does not replace them. Thus, Ireland, the UK, and Germany actually have privacy regulations that were already in place. Organizations that had worked to be in compliance with their existing country regulations had fewer modifications to their policies to make.

One of the biggest impacts of EU GDPR is that it encompasses non-EU organizations. Any organization that maintains PII on EU data subjects has to be in compliance or face fines and other regulatory actions. A data subject is any person whose residence is in an EU country. That includes travelers, tourists, and employees on temporary assignment to an EU country. Thus, practically every global company falls under its purview.

The immediate unintended consequence was that many companies, particularly subscription news services, blocked access from the EU to their services. Imagine a new app being launched by a small team of developers. Their business plan may have been based on inline ads and growing a subscriber list. They would not be able to show compliance with GDPR and would take the simple route of allowing downloads only from non-EU countries.

GDPR creates an enforcement infrastructure consisting of data protection authorities and data protection supervisors in each country. It requires that every organization assign the sole role of data protection officer (DPO) to a single person. The DPO is the main point of contact with the country's data protection supervisor. The duties of the DPO are to demonstrate compliance to the supervisor and notify the supervisor within 72 hours of a data breach. That requirement alone is problematic for most organizations as they have historically taken much longer than three days to even determine that a breach has occurred.

Keep in mind that in several places GDPR calls for the use of "state-of-the-art security." This all-encompassing requirement could be difficult to demonstrate if enforcement measures are taken.

These are other terms that need defining to understand GDPR:

- **Data Controller**: This is the organization that decides what data needs to be collected and for what purpose. There is a tendency to collect as much data on a subscriber or individual as possible. An employer may want to know everything about a job applicant, for instance, including Twitter handles, Facebook pages, and LinkedIn profiles. GDPR attempts to minimize this data collection.

- **Data Processor**: This is any third party that stores, organizes, or in any way interacts with the collected data. Think cloud and SaaS services.

### 5.2.1.1    The Right to Erasure

Article 17 of GDPR is often referred to, incorrectly, as the *right to be forgotten*. It certainly had its origins in the European movement for the "right to be forgotten," which began when an EU citizen complained that the first page of results on a Google search of his name included news reports of something bad he had done in the past. He sued Google over it as if Google was malevolently trying to sully his good name. Think of what a search engine has to do to comply with such a request. Google's algorithm for ranking search results is secret, but we know a lot about what it looks at to determine where a result resides. The page rank of the sites has a big impact. How often people click through to the result may also be taken into consideration. To comply, Google may have to write code that searches for the score of particular pages that give the offending result and deprecate them. Of course, if compelled to do such a thing, Google would be reducing the value of its search engine, as its results would not include the most salient information.

All that said, Article 17 of GDPR provides for a method of redress for data subjects in the EU. With the expected exceptions for law enforcement, healthcare providers, and any other legal or regulatory domain, an organization that collects or processes personally identifiable information on any EU subjects must build the systems to do the following:

- Accept and respond to requests for all the data in its possession that may be associated with the data subject. This means any one of 300 million people can submit a request to any organization that has their name, email, phone number, residence, age, sex, height, weight, or any data that can be identified with the individual. The organization, usually a commercial organization, must respond within 90 days or face fines and other enforcement actions. Somewhat ironically, the response, be it on a secured website or simply an emailed response with a file containing all of the data, creates a new copy of the data that may have to be secured against theft or leakage.

- Respond to a data subject that wants the organization to erase all of the data about the individual by actually erasing all of the person's data from all of its records.

GDPR went into effect on May 25, 2017. Like all regulations, ambiguous language is ultimately interpreted, either in civil courts, or a norm is created by the agencies that must enforce it. GDPR is rife with such ambiguities. In two articles GDPR requires organizations to use "state-of-the-art security" to protect data. The following is a discussion of what would actually have to occur if a data subject's information were truly to be erased. Thankfully, at least initially, most countries are interpreting GDPR's requirements in a much more lenient manner.

To put the following discussion in context, first think of all the organizations that may collect, store, and process personally identifiable information:

- Financial institutions. Think of anyplace you may provide data to maintain an account such as your bank, stock trading sites, retirement savings accounts, your mortgage broker and holder, and all of the lenders you may have applied to for business or personal loan. Under GDPR these could be headquartered anywhere in the world, although for enforcement they probably have to have enough business in your country of residence to warrant prosecution if they fail to comply.

- Marketing organizations that collect, maintain, and sell mailing lists for direct mail or email.

- Any retailer that has a loyalty program.

- Any online retailer you have ever used to order products.

- Subscription websites.
- Your email provider, be it Yahoo!, Microsoft, Gmail, or Hotmail.
- Your hosting provider for your website.
- Any app you have downloaded to your smartphone.
- The list goes on. Note that it includes practically the entire universe of digital services and products.

Now consider what has to happen to completely erase a data subject's information for the systems maintained by a data collector or processor.

Records are collected in some way. Research organizations may scrape websites like LinkedIn for complete biographical information. Organizations may purchase information from resellers of this data. They may even come into possession of the information when they acquire another company. Often the information is even included in the calculation of the acquired company's value. Most often, the data subject provides the information freely in exchange for some perceived value. They enter a contest or sign up for a newsletter or a "free" subscription to a website.

While a small organization may store its customer lists or subscriber lists in a file or spreadsheet, it is much more common for data to be stored in a relational database. A request to fully erase data from a database poses some overwhelming problems.

Imagine a database with millions of records. For simplicity, imagine that data is full name, address, age, sex, email address, and telephone number. This would fall within the purview of GDPR and be subject to erasure upon request. That data resides in a database. The records of a database are not just a flat file. They are distributed across multiple hard drives (most likely SSDs in a modern cloud deployment), which are redundantly configured in a RAID array. When a record is deleted from a database, all of the pointers maintained by the relational database software are simply marked as "deleted." A search on the record will not divulge the deleted records. But, much like consigning a file to the trash bin on a computer, the actual data is not overwritten. A forensic analysis of the storage medium would reveal the data. It may be difficult (expensive) to reconstruct an entire record, but not impossible.

Assume that Hans Schmidt, an EU resident, requests that his information be erased from the database of a company where he used to have an account. The company would look up his record in their application, the front end to the database, and delete it. Most databases log all access and actions, including the data that is entered or retrieved. In other words, there is another copy of Hans' data in the database logs! It is often possible to rebuild an entire database from logs alone.

Most databases are backed up continuously. The live backup would quickly inherit the version that did not contain Hans' information. But long-term backups may exist in multiple versions, either on disk or written to tape.

Now imagine that immediately after Han's records are deleted and Hans is notified that they have complied with his request, a glitch occurs. The IT staff scrambles to recover from the glitch—a power outage, an earthquake, a ransomware attack—and they restore the most recent copy of the database. Hans, in doing a Google search discovers that his information is still available from the company. From the regulator's perspective not only has the company failed to comply with Hans' request, but it falsely claimed it had!

If the right to erasure were interpreted to mean that data had to be fully sanitized, there are several steps that may be required.

One method proposed is to delete Hans' data, create a new copy of the entire database that would not include Hans' data, and then sanitize the storage medium used for the original copy. Hans' data would be gone forever, except, of course, from previous backups of the database or the logs. Although effective, this method would be extremely onerous for a company to build into their processes.

A simpler approach has been proposed:

1. Overwrite all of the fields containing Hans' data with the same number of bits. This may entail overwriting text and number fields with the same number of alphanumeric characters in the same language. This assumes the database software assigns the new information to the same locations in the storage media.

2. Delete the record.

Now the only place Han's information can be recovered is in the backups and logs. The same operations could be performed on them.

As mentioned, luckily for all data controllers and processors who are subject to enforcement actions under GDPR, the norm that was quickly established for compliance with Article 17 is simple: after erasure, the data subject's information is not visible to any user. In other words, the data subject cannot find it, an auditor cannot find it, and even a data thief cannot find it if they get access to the database.

For now, the best practice, possibly even the "state of the art," is to maintain a complete data sanitization program that will prevent Hans' data from showing up on hard drives or backup tapes that make their way to the aftermarket or a landfill.

For data sanitization, the following are the relevant portions of the 457-page GDPR regulation:

### Article 1, Section 17 Right to Erasure

*1. "The data subject shall have the right to obtain from the controller the erasure of personal data concerning him or her without undue delay and the controller shall have the obligation to erase personal data without undue delay where one of the following grounds applies: (a) the personal data are no longer necessary in relation to the purposes for which they were collected or otherwise processed;*

*(b) the data subject withdraws consent on which the processing is based according to point (a) of Article 6(1), or point (a) of Article 9(2), and where there is no other legal ground for the processing; (c) the data subject objects to the processing pursuant to*

*Article 21(1) and there are no overriding legitimate grounds for the processing, or the data subject objects to the processing pursuant to Article 21(2);*

*(d) the personal data have been unlawfully processed;*

*(e) the personal data have to be erased for compliance with a legal obligation in Union or Member State law to which the controller is*

*subject; (f) the personal data have been collected in relation to the offer of*

*information society services referred to in Article 8(1)."*

The right to erasure creates a requirement to be able to provide proof of erasure for eventual audits by the data protection supervisor. Have records accessible and tied to the requests for erasure from data subjects. These records should be easily accessible and linked to any requests for erasure.

### Article 13: Information to the Data Subject

*1. Where personal data relating to a data subject are collected from the data subject, the controller shall, at the time when*

*personal data are obtained, provide the data subject with all of the*

*following information:*

*(a) the identity and the contact details of the controller and, where*

*applicable, of the controller's representative;*

*(b) the contact details of the data protection officer, where applicable;*

*(c) the purposes of the processing for which the personal data are*

*intended as well as the legal basis for the processing;*

*(d) where the processing is based on point... the legitimate*

*interests pursued by the controller or by a third party;*

*(e) the recipients or categories of recipients of the personal data, if any;*

*(f) where applicable, the fact that the controller intends to transfer*

*personal data to a third country or international organization*

*and the existence or absence of an adequacy decision by*

*the Commission, or in the case of transfers...reference to the*

*appropriate or suitable safeguards and the means by which to*

*obtain a copy of them or where they have been made available.*

*2. ...[T]he controller shall, at the time when personal data are*

*obtained, provide the data subject with the following further*

*information necessary to ensure fair and transparent processing:*

*(a) the period for which the personal data will be stored, or if that is*

*not possible, the criteria used to determine that period;*

*(b) the existence of the right to request from the controller access*

*to and rectification or erasure of personal data or restriction*

*of processing concerning the data subject or to object to*

*processing as well as the right to data portability;*

*(c) where the processing is based on point...the existence of the right*

*to withdraw consent at any time, without affecting the lawfulness of*

*processing based on consent before its withdrawal [...]*

*3. Where the controller intends to further process the personal*

*data for a purpose other than that for which the personal data*

*were collected, the controller shall provide the data subject prior*

*to that further processing with information on that other purpose*

*and with any relevant further information [...]."*

This section gives you an idea of the specificity of GDPR and the need to create a policy and team to ensure compliance. When the purpose for which data is collected expires, ensure data location is tracked and available for erasure. Keep tamper-proof records of compliance with this requirement.

**39**

*"...Personal data should be processed only if the purpose of*

*the processing could not reasonably be fulfilled by other means.*

*In order to ensure that the personal data are not kept longer than*

*necessary, time limits should be established by the controller for*

*erasure or for a periodic review. Every reasonable step should*

*be taken to ensure that personal data which are inaccurate are*

*rectified or deleted."*

Inaccurate data, if not corrected, should be securely erased and a tamper-proof (digitally signed) record kept of the action.

### 5.2.1.2  Data Retention

This is the relevant text to data retention:

**Chapter 3, Section 3, Article 19**

*Notification obligation regarding rectification or erasure of*

*personal data or restriction of processing*

*"The controller shall communicate any rectification or erasure of*

*personal data or restriction of processing carried out in accordance*

*with Articles 16, 17(1) and 18 to each recipient to whom the personal*

*data have been disclosed, unless this proves impossible or involves*

*disproportionate effort. The controller shall inform the data subject*

*about those recipients if the data subject requests it."*

Provide a certificate of erasure to the data subject, a tamper-proof digitally signed document.

**Chapter 1, Section 5, Article 25**

*Data protection by design and by default*

*1. "[...] the controller shall, both at the time of the determination of*

*the means for processing and at the time of the processing itself,*

*implement appropriate technical and organizational measures, such as pseudonymisation, which are designed to implement*

*data-protection principles, such as data minimization, in an*

*effective manner and to integrate the necessary safeguards*

*into the processing in order to meet the requirements of this*

*Regulation and protect the rights of data subjects.*

*2. The controller shall implement appropriate technical and*

*organizational measures for ensuring that, by default, only*

*personal data which are necessary for each specific purpose*

*of the processing are processed. That obligation applies to the*

*amount of personal data collected, the extent of their processing,*

*the period of their storage and their accessibility. In particular,*

*such measures shall ensure that by default personal data are*

*not made accessible without the individual's intervention to an*

*indefinite number of natural persons."*

"By design and by default" implies processes throughout the lifecycle of the data. Be able to demonstrate that the end of life of data is planned for and procedures are in place to securely erase the data.

**Article 30**

**Records of Processing Activities**

*1. "Each controller and, where applicable, the controller's*

*representative, shall maintain a record of processing activities*

*under its responsibility. That record shall contain all of the*

*following information:*

*(a) the name and contact details of the controller and, where*

*applicable, the joint controller, the controller's representative and*

*the data protection officer;*

*(b) the purposes of the processing;*

*(c) a description of the categories of data subjects and of the*

*categories of personal data;*

*(d) the categories of recipients to whom the personal data have*

*been or will be disclosed including recipients in third countries or*

*international organisations;*

*...(f) where possible, the envisaged time limits for erasure of the*

*different categories of data [...]"*

Add the data controller's contact details to the certified erasure reports.

## 5.2.2    HIPAA Security Rule Subpart C

The Health Insurance Portability and Accountability Act (HIPAA) went into effect August 21, 1996. It is of particular concern for hospitals, doctors' offices, health insurers, and any organization that handles healthcare records in the United States. Fines and enforcement actions fall under the U.S. Department of Health and Human Services (HSS). HHS can refer violations to the Department of Justice for criminal prosecution.

### § 164.306 Security standards: General rules

*(B) Risk management*

*(Required).*

*Implement security measures sufficient*

*to reduce risks and vulnerabilities to*

*a reasonable and appropriate level to*

*comply with § 164.306(a).*

*(D) Information system activity review*

*(Required). Implement procedures to*

*regularly review records of information*

*system activity, such as audit logs,*

*access reports and security incident*

*tracking reports.*

Among the other forms of keeping logs, an organization should track data erasure events.

### § 164.308 Administrative safeguards

*(1)(i) Standard: Security management*

*process. Implement policies and*

*procedures to prevent, detect, contain*

*and correct security violations.*

Data sanitization should be incorporated in overall security management policies. Note that HIPAA does not explicitly mention data erasure or sanitization.

### 164.314 Organizational requirements

*(i) Business associate contracts. The*

*contract between a covered entity and*

*a business associate must provide*

*that the business associate will— (A)*

*Implement administrative, physical, and*

*technical safeguards that reasonably and*

*appropriately protect the confidentiality,*

*integrity, and availability of the electronic*

*protected health information that it*

*creates, receives, maintains, or transmits*

*on behalf of the covered entity as*

*required by this subpart.*

Ensure that third parties that may process electronic protected health information have data sanitization policies in place and the technology and processes to fulfill them.

### § 164.314 Organizational requirements

*(i) Implement administrative, physical, and*

*technical safeguards that reasonably and*

*appropriately protect the confidentiality,*

*integrity, and availability of the electronic*

*protected health information that it*

*creates, receives, maintains, or transmits*

*on behalf of the group health plan*

Safeguards should include data sanitization methods for end of life and temporary usage of health records.

### § 164.316 Policies and procedures

*(i) Time limit (Required). Retain the*

*documentation required by paragraph (b)*

*(1) of this section for 6 years from the date*

*of its creation or the date when it last was*

*in effect, whichever is later.*

Limit liability by ensuring proper data sanitization at the end of the required retention period of six years. Record all data sanitization events.

### § 164.504 Uses and disclosures:

*Organizational requirements.*

*(ii) Provide that the business associate*

*will:*

*(I) At termination of the contract, if*

*feasible, return or destroy all protected*

*health information received from, or*

*created or received by the business*

*associate on behalf of, the covered*

*entity that the business associate still*

*maintains in any form and retain no*

*copies of such information or, if such*

*return or destruction is not feasible,*

*extend the protections of the contract*

*to the information and limit further uses*

*and disclosures to those purposes that*

*make the return or destruction of the*

*information infeasible.*

This is the most direct HIPAA requirement to destroy protected health information. It requires that proper data sanitization methods be used to destroy all protected data. Provide a tamper-proof record of destruction to demonstrate compliance.

### § 164.504 Uses and disclosures:

*Organizational requirements.*

*(I) If feasible, return or destroy all*

*protected health information received*

*from the group health plan that the*

*sponsor still maintains in any form and*

*retain no copies of such information*

*when no longer needed for the purpose*

*for which disclosure was made, except*

*that, if such return or destruction is not*

*feasible, limit further uses and disclosures*

*to those purposes that make the return or*

*destruction.*

Use proper data sanitization methods to destroy all protected data. Provide a tamper-proof record of destruction to demonstrate compliance.

## 5.2.3    PCI DSS V3.2 Payment Card Industry Requirements

In 2004, the major credit card brands got together to issue version 1.0 of the Payment Card Industry Data Security Standard (PCI DSS). PCI DSS is unique in that it explicitly addresses security requirements for any organization that wants to accept credit card payments or process payments on behalf of merchants. It was the first security standard to have a direct impact on a large number of companies. It did not come with regulatory fines or other actions by a government agency or law enforcement. It is an industry standard. Failure to comply can result in a merchant or processor being banned from accepting credit cards.

The sections of the version of PCI DSS that can be interpreted as data sanitization requirements follow:

**3 .1**

*Keep cardholder data storage to a minimum*

*by implementing data retention and disposal*

*policies, procedures and processes that*

*include at least the following for all cardholder*

*data (CHD) storage:*

*Limiting data storage amount and retention*

*time to that which is required for legal,*

*regulatory, and/or business requirements*

*Specific retention requirements for*

*cardholder data*

*Processes for secure deletion of data*

*when no longer needed*

*A quarterly process for identifying and*

*securely deleting stored cardholder data*

*that exceeds defined retention*

Link data retention periods to data sanitization processes. Use proper data sanitization methods to destroy all card holder data. Provide a tamper-proof record of destruction to demonstrate compliance.

**3.2**

*Do not store sensitive authentication*

*data after authorization (even if encrypted).*

*If sensitive authentication data is received,*

*render all data unrecoverable upon completion*

*of the authorization process.*

*It is permissible for issuers and companies*

*that support issuing services to store sensitive*

*authentication data if:*

*There is a business justification and*

*The data is stored securely*

Apply data sanitization to all card holder records as soon as authorization is complete.

**9.8.2**

*Render cardholder data on electronic*

*media unrecoverable so that cardholder data*

*cannot be reconstructed.*

Use secure overwrite to ensure cardholder data cannot be forensically recovered.

**10.7**

*Retain audit trail history for at least*

*one year, with a minimum of three months*

*immediately available for analysis (for example,*

*online, archived or restorable from backup)*

Store all tamper-proof records of erasure in an easily retrievable format.

## 5.2.4   Sarbanes–Oxley

In the aftermath of the business failure of publicly traded Enron, the U.S. Congress quickly passed the Public Company Accounting Reform and Investor Protection Act, commonly known as Sarbanes–Oxley. Enacted in 2002, this act called for significant accounting reform and included references to keeping data and systems secure. It also made senior executives responsible for oversight and security.

Sarbanes–Oxley makes only one demand that could be interpreted in terms of data sanitization:

*§ 1520. Destruction of corporate audit records, requires audit records, notes, etc. to be kept for at least five years.*

Limit liability and discovery expenses by applying data destruction to records after the required retention period of five years.

## 5.2.5    Saudi Arabian Monetary Authority Payment Services Regulations

The Saudi Arabian Monetary Authority (SAMA)Payment Services Regulation was issued in early 2020. Among its requirements are the following:

---

**"Information assets should be disposed of in accordance with legal and regulatory requirements, when no longer required (i.e. meeting data privacy regulations to avoid unauthorized access and avoid (un)intended data leakage)."**

---

Data sanitization should be applied to media at the end of its useful life and to records.

---

**"Sensitive information should be destroyed using techniques to make the information non-retrievable (e.g., secure erase, secure wiping, incineration, double crosscut, shredding)."**

---

Use appropriate data sanitization with full records of destruction.

---

**"The Member Organization should ensure that third party service providers used for secure disposal, transport and storage comply with the secure disposal standard and procedure and the effectiveness is periodically measured and evaluated."**

---

Third-party data sanitization providers should provide auditable records of every destruction action in tamper-proof digitally signed documents.

## 5.2.6    New York State Cybersecurity Requirements of Financial Services Companies 23 NYCRR 500

Effective March 1, 2017, the Superintendent of Financial Services of the State of New York published 23 NYCRR Part 500, a regulation establishing cybersecurity requirements for financial services companies. New York is the home of many of the largest financial services companies in the world. Many global financial companies have divisions in New York too. Compliance with these requirements include the following requirements related to data sanitization:

*Section 500.13 Limitations on Data Retention. As part of its cybersecurity program, each Covered Entity shall include policies and procedures for the secure*

*disposal on a periodic basis of any Nonpublic Information*

*identified in section 500.01(g)(2)-(3) of this Part that is no longer necessary for business operations or for other legitimate business purposes of the Covered Entity, except where such information is otherwise required to be retained by law or regulation, or where targeted disposal is not reasonably feasible due to the manner in which the information is maintained.*

Demonstrate compliance by creating and enforcing a data sanitization policy.

## 5.2.7    Philippines Data Privacy Act 2012

Compliance is often treated as an academic exercise of good management and attention to detail. The threat of fines and other regulatory actions is used to justify putting controls and record keeping in place. The 2012 Data Privacy Act enacted in the Philippines deviates from the other regulations cited so far in that it imposes jail time for infractions.

**Chapter VIII SEC. 27. Improper Disposal of Personal Information and Sensitive Personal Information**

*(a) The improper disposal of personal information shall be penalized by imprisonment ranging from six (6) months to two (2) years and a fine of not less than One hundred thousand pesos (Php100,000.00) but not more than Five hundred thousand pesos (Php500,000.00) shall be imposed on persons who knowingly or negligently dispose, discard or abandon the personal information of an individual in an area accessible to the public or has otherwise placed the personal information of an individual in its container for trash collection.*

Avoid these harsh penalties by implementing a data sanitization policy that identifies personal information, its purpose for collection, and its entire lifecycle up to final destruction.

**Chap IV Rights of the Data Subject**

*e) Suspend, withdraw or order the blocking, removal or destruction of his or her personal information from the personal information controller's filing system upon discovery and substantial proof that the personal information are incomplete, outdated, false, unlawfully obtained, used for unauthorized purposes or are no longer necessary for the purposes for which they were collected. In this case, the personal information controller may notify third parties who have previously received such processed personal information;*

Be able to provide proof of erasure for eventual audits by data protection regulators. The records should be accessible and tied to the requests for erasure from data subjects.

## 5.2.8   Singapore Personal Data Protection Act 2012

As this litany of country regulations for data privacy is laid out, the arguments for having an information security management program are reinforced. As can be seen, an organization that has operations in multiple countries will have many separate compliance requirements. An overarching data sanitization program that meets the requirements of each country will be easier to implement and manage than separate programs for each region. With the proper handling of data, it should be possible to discover and protect all of the data that falls under each regulation and quickly produce reports to demonstrate compliance to auditors.

### Part VI Retention of personal data

*25. An organisation shall cease to retain its documents containing personal data, or remove the means by which the personal data can be associated with particular individuals, as soon as it is reasonable to assume that —*

*(a)the purpose for which that personal data was collected is no longer being served by retention of the personal data; and*

*(b)retention is no longer necessary for legal or business purposes.*

Be able to provide proof of erasure for eventual audits by the data protection supervisor. Have them accessible and tied to the requests for erasure from data subjects.

## 5.2.9   Gramm–Leach–Bliley Act

Gramm–Leach–Bliley Act (GLBA) is a regulation that pertains to financial institutions in the United States. Its primary purpose was to remove restrictions on the combination of different types of financial institutions. It paved the way for banks to merge with insurance companies, for instance. It also required every financial company to issue a privacy notice to every customer.

*Article 682.3 - Proper disposal of consumer information-*

*states that "Any person who maintains or otherwise*

*possesses consumer information for a business purpose*

*must properly dispose of such information by taking*

*reasonable measures to protect against unauthorized*

*access to or use of the information in connection with its* disposal." In this instance, "disposal" refers to the "discarding or abandonment of consumer information" or "The sale,

donation, or transfer of any medium, including computer

equipment, upon which consumer information is stored."

The article also states that *"Reasonable measures*

*to protect against unauthorized access to or use of*

*consumer information in connection with its disposal*

*include... implementing and monitoring compliance with*

*policies and procedures that require the destruction*

*or erasure of electronic media containing consumer*

*information so that the information cannot practicably be*

*read or reconstructed."*

## 5.3   Standards

### 5.3.1   ISO 27000 and Family

The ISO 27000 series of standards evolved from BSI 7799 first published in 1995. It is widely used around the world as the framework for information security management systems (ISMSs). It is high-level in that it does not specify security controls as much as specify that controls must exist and be documented.

One section of ISO 27000 pertains to data sanitization.

**A.11.2 Equipment**

*A.11.2.7 Secure disposal or reuse of equipment*

*Control*

*All items of equipment containing storage media*

*shall be verified to ensure that any sensitive*

*data and licensed software has been removed or*

*securely overwritten prior to disposal or re-use.*

Note that this section requires a data sanitization policy to implement.

The ISO/IEC 27040:2015 standard provides detailed technical guidance on data storage security including the proper disposal of data storage media. It aligns with NIST 800-88 by providing definitions of destruct, purge, and sanitize.

## 5.3.2    NIST SP 800-88

The U.S. National Institute of Standards and Testing published the Special Publication 800-88 Revision 1, "Guidelines for Media Sanitization," in December 2014. According to the preamble, "Media sanitization refers to a process that renders access to target data on the media infeasible for a given level of effort."

In section 2.1, the special publication goes on to say:

> **"In order for organizations to have appropriate controls on the information they are responsible for safeguarding, they must properly safeguard used media. An often rich source of illicit information collection is either through dumpster diving for improperly disposed hard copy media, acquisition of improperly sanitized electronic media, or through keyboard and laboratory reconstruction of media sanitized in a manner not commensurate with the confidentiality of its information."**

NIST states explicitly the following:

> **"For storage devices containing *magnetic* media, a single overwrite pass with a fixed pattern such as binary zeros typically hinders recovery of data even if state of the art laboratory techniques are applied to attempt to retrieve the data."**

When it comes to degaussing, the publication points out this:

> **"...because some emerging variations of magnetic recording technologies incorporate media with higher coercivity (magnetic force). As a result, existing degaussers may not have sufficient force to effectively degauss such media." See more on the problems associated with coercivity in new storage methods like thermal and microwave enhanced writing to disks, see the chapter on the Future of Data Sanitization.**

Section 2.6 points out the efficiency and speed of crypto-erase: because the data on a self-encrypting drive is already encrypted, it can be sanitized in a fraction of a second by just sanitizing the keys. (Note: there have been reported cases of manufacturers shipping self-encrypting drives with the encryption turned off or the keys easily recoverable from the drive. Thus, even crypto-erased drives should be verified.)

NIST 800-88 depends on categorizing the security classification of data. The following flowchart depicts a decision tree of how to sanitize data based on

Low, Medium, and High security categorizations. Within federal agencies, this type of categorization is normal, but most organizations have not implemented such a program.

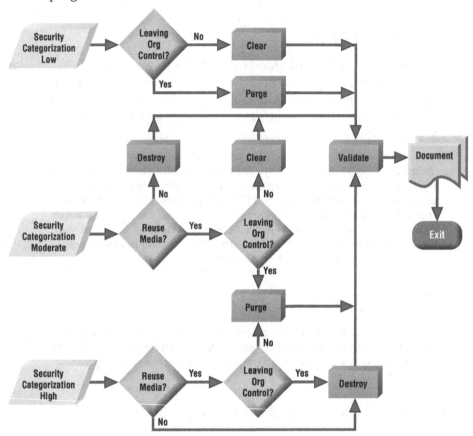

Note that the final stages are: verify and document.

Most ITADs cannot make the determination of the value or category of data, so they treat it all the same and seek to sanitize all media completely.

The following are the records that should be kept when a device is sanitized:

- Manufacturer
- Model
- Serial number
- Organizationally assigned media or property number (if applicable) and media type (i.e., magnetic, flash memory, hybrid, etc.)
- Media source (i.e., user or computer the media came from)
- Pre-sanitization confidentiality categorization (optional)
- Sanitization description (i.e., clear, purge, destroy)

- Method used (i.e., degauss, overwrite, block erase, crypto-erase, etc.) and tool used (including version)
- Verification method (i.e., full, quick sampling, etc.)
- Post-sanitization confidentiality categorization (optional)
- Post-sanitization destination (if known)

For both sanitization and verification, the following should be kept:

- Name of person
- Position/title of person
- Date
- Location
- Phone or other contact information or signature

There is apparently no plan to update NIST SP 800-88, which is eight years old. That is part of the motivation of IEEE to create a new standard for media sanitization. Note that the e-Stewards Standard cites SP 800-88 for its data sanitization requirements (or, a more stringent national standard, if it exists).

## 5.4   Summary

NIST may not be planning to update its standard for media sanitization, but there are plenty of other organizations that see a need for improved standards. The evolution of technology, the growth of data, the number of new devices with data on them, and the rise of new products like wearables for medical monitoring, as well as new storage technologies, are going to need guides for data sanitization. The next chapter introduces new standards that are being developed to address this need. It is important to keep an eye on standards that are in the process of being published because they may impact your own data sanitization procedures.

# New Standards

There is no better indicator of the rising importance of effective data sanitization than the activity from standards bodies. Both the Institute of Electrical and Electronics Engineers (IEEE) and the International Standards Organization (ISO) are introducing new data sanitization standards. While NIST Special Publication 800-88 provided good direction when it was originally published and served to clear up the need for many overwrite passes, it is generally considered to be in dire need of an update.

Always keep in mind that standards usually precede regulations by several years. As regulatory agencies seek to impose more data rules in the future, they may incorporate these standards as a requirement. If you are building out your own data sanitization policies, responsibilities, workflows, and audit requirements, starting with these standards will help you be in line with future industry or government requirements.

# 6.1   IEEE P2883 Draft Standard for Sanitizing Storage

The proposed IEEE P2883 Standard for Sanitizing Storage is in its 15th draft as we go to press and is out for public comment. Note that the new standard is focused on hardware, not data. Data center operators, manufacturers, and ITADs share this hardware focus, so the standard provides excellent guidance for them.

The preamble to the new standard states:

> **"A wide variety of data types are recorded on a range of data storage technologies. When these systems or their media are repurposed or retired from use, access to the recorded data often must be eliminated (sanitized) to avoid unauthorized access to the data. Depending on the storage technology, specific methods must be employed to ensure that the data are either eliminated or the logical storage and physical storage associated with the data devices/media are disposed of properly."**

Drilling into hardware sanitization requirements is important because storage media evolves quickly to be faster, cheaper, and denser. We talk about future storage technology in the last chapter of this book.

The standard goes on to define three interpretations of the term *sanitization*.

## 6.1.1   Data Sanitization

Data sanitization is focused on all instances of stored data, wherever the data resides. Such elimination can be quite challenging because all copies need to be identified, and adequate data maps may or may not exist. These data copies can exist within applications, cloud services, virtual environments, primary compute and storage resources, secondary and offline storage, archives, and data protection systems (e.g., backups and replications). For each of these data locations, specific technology-oriented actions (to achieve storage sanitization) are then necessary to eliminate the data.

## 6.1.2   Storage Sanitization

Storage sanitization is focused on data stored on ICT infrastructure that uses nonvolatile storage (e.g., fixed-block storage arrays, NAS systems, object storage, cloud storage, and backup systems) that can take the form of logical/virtual storage or media-aligned storage.

## 6.1.3   Media Sanitization

Media sanitization is focused on data stored on storage devices or storage media.

Then, 2883 defines the difference between *clear*, *purge*, and *destruct*.

## 6.1.4   Clear

Clear is a sanitization method that uses logical techniques on all addressable storage locations for protection against simple noninvasive data recovery techniques using the same host interface available to the user.

Logical techniques are the overwriting possible with commands sent from the host or the reset comments for SSDs.

The standard notes, "Clear is not appropriate for sensitive data because Clear is not required to remove data from addressable locations."

## 6.1.5   Purge

Purge is a sanitization method that uses logical techniques or physical techniques that make recovery of target data infeasible using state-of-the-art laboratory techniques applied to an intact or disassembled storage device, but that preserves the storage media and the storage device in a potentially reusable state.

## 6.1.6   Destruct

Destruct is a sanitization method that makes recovery of target data infeasible using state-of-the-art laboratory techniques and results in the subsequent inability to use the storage media.

The standard includes these destruction methods: disintegration, incineration, and melting.

Controversially, the standard has deprecated shredding and pulverization because it claims that storage densities have made it possible to recover data even from the smallest shard of a CD or hard disk platter. The authors know of no research or lab demonstrations of data recovery techniques from even large shards of a disk platter. It is possible to imagine such techniques. For instance, you could use machine vision to virtually assemble the shards into their original configuration and then read the data off each track on each fragment and reassemble all the original data. Perhaps the authors of the standard are privy to unpublished capabilities of intelligence agencies. This dramatic interpretation of destruction requirements will disrupt the operations of thousands of recycling facilities (ITADs) that use R2, eStewards, or other practical standards for destruction. R2v3, for instance, calls for shredding hard drives into fragments and pulverizing SSDs. Typically the fragment sizes possible with modern shredders is 20X20 mm. Pulverizing SSDs can leave 2×2 mm granules. Additional protection against recovery can be provided by mixing the fragments with other fragments.

ITADs immediately mix the fragments in with millions of other fragments. This makes the reassembly and discovery of data too expensive even for an intelligence agency to undertake today.

## 6.2 Updated ISO/IEC CD 27040 Information Technology Security Techniques—Storage Security[*]

While the IEEE P2883 standard explains how to sanitize various media, the ISO/IEC CD 27040 currently under development will describe *when* to sanitize.

The current version of this standard is ISO/IEC 27040:2015. Annex A of the standard aligns its data sanitization approach with that of NIST 800-88. This standard, which also covers other aspects of storage security, is reviewed every five years.

Because of the transformation in data storage over the past decade, going from more isolated connectivity and physical/geographic protections to remote, virtual, and cloud-based architectures, the updated standard will take a more system-centric approach, supporting information security management system (ISMS) requirements according to ISO/IEC 27001, including logical and cloud storage.

From a sanitization perspective, the ISO/IEC 27040 draft is radically different from the published standard. For one thing, most of the device-specific language has been removed. In addition, the draft defers to IEEE 2883, outlined earlier— rather than NIST—when recommending how specific types of media or logical storage can be sanitized and which sanitization methods to use.

One of the more important aspects of the revision is the inclusion of multiple "shall" statements, giving clear requirements and actions when determining which points in an asset's lifecycle (e.g., maintenance, disposal) require sanitization, what constitutes compliance including minimal acceptable conditions for using cryptographic erasure, and what constitutes proof, or record, of satisfactory sanitization.

The update to ISO/IEC 27040 also broadens its instructions on confirming a particular data sanitization method has been achieved.

For instance, while maintaining the clear, purge, and destruct framework, it refines the verification/validation aspect of NIST 800-88 as it relates to physical destruction: "destruct" verification should kick off a physical evaluation of the final condition of destroyed materials. This inspection—of shard size, for example—will help organizations weigh the cost and necessity of taking further action such as additional shredding to protect the most sensitive data.

The updated content also aligns with the new ISO/IEC 27002, which adds controls for NVMe-oF technology and Intelligent Platform Management Interface (IPMI) specifications, and includes a new scheme for identifying requirements and guidance.

---

[*]This section adapted from the Data Sanitization Consortium article at www.datasanitization .org/device-sanitization-standards-are-changing-iso-27040-ieee- p2883.

The revision, under development by the ISO/IEC JTC 1/SC27 Information Security, Cybersecurity, and Privacy Protection Technical Committee, is scheduled to be completed after P2883 is published, enabling the two standards to work together.

## 6.3    Summary

You can see that the old saying that states "the best thing about standards is that there are so many to choose from" is playing out in this arena too. You have to determine which standard is most closely aligned with your region and industry. Following a standard and even being certified to a particular standard can be a good defense in court if you want to demonstrate "best practices" or even "state of the art." You also have to keep an eye on future standards and regulations that are being formulated for your industry.

We have built a case for creating a data sanitization program across your organization. It may be driven by regulatory compliance requirements or by security and privacy needs. The next chapters can help you formalize your policies and a manageable process for creating and maintaining a data sanitization program.

# Asset Lifecycle Management

## 7.1 Data Sanitization Program

For most organizations, employee computers (including desktops, laptops, and tablets) pose the most pressing need for a defined data sanitization program. The fear of an embarrassing or damaging leak occurring because one of these devices ends up in the wrong hands is usually what sparks the creation of such a program. Many organizations with an IT department of one or two people may have a closet full of old clunky laptops and tower computers just because the fear is there but the program for processing them has not been initiated. Perhaps they even use DBAN (Darik's Boot and Nuke) to erase them and then list them for sale on eBay, or donate them to charity. Office-supply chains have computer disposal services. Even the Salvation Army will collect old computers. Sometimes these organizations turn them over to an ITAD, which will pay either the charity or the office-supply store something for the residual value.

In general, businesses should incorporate the services of an ITAD in their equipment disposal processes.

A data sanitization program should be kicked off with several steps:

1. Create a policy. An appropriate policy is based on: "All devices that contain organization data will be sanitized before leaving the control of the organization."

2. Identify the types of devices. This list will include the following:

   ▪ Desktops

   ▪ Laptops

   ▪ Tablets

   ▪ Servers (mail, print, file, application, database)

   ▪ Storage (NAS, loose hard drives, thumb drives)

   ▪ Phones and PBXs

   ▪ Printers

   ▪ Copiers

   ▪ Cell phones

   ▪ IoT devices such as CC TVs, PLCs, and plant floor computers

3. Specify the process for each category of devices.

4. Define how the process will be verified for audit.

## 7.2   Laptops and Desktops

For laptops, desktops, and tablets, the process starts with scheduling a device to be taken out of service. The owner typically turns it in when they are issued a new device. Often this is an ongoing process, but sometimes an organization-wide update may occur when the budget is finally freed up to transition from

Windows XP, for instance. Yes, there are still many large organizations using unsupported versions of Windows. When a device is decommissioned, there should be a process of recording the fact. An asset identifier, if present, should be recorded and the device labeled or otherwise marked for disposal.

The devices scheduled for disposal should be kept in a secure area (the afore-mentioned closet or a storage cage). Access to the secure area must be restricted and records of access kept. Ask yourself if you can trace the ownership (who has control of the device) throughout its life. If a data breach is ever traced to a user or device, can you produce documents to prove when it slipped through the cracks of your process?

Before any device leaves your control, it should be sanitized. A software overwrite should be performed and an immutable record created of the data sanitization. That record should contain the device identifier (asset tag, serial number of computer and of the hard drive), the method used to overwrite (standard used, number of passes, what kind of passes such as random or blocks of ones and zeros), and any failures to overwrite particular sectors. If too many disk sectors fail or the entire overwrite process is not possible, then the device should be treated separately. If possible, the storage should be removed, and physical destruction should take place. Many large organizations have mechanical shredders or degaussers for this purpose. Or a contracted third party can provide shredding services.

Finally, a record in the form of a receipt should be kept when the device is passed on to a third party.

An organization with several hundred employees may implement this process effectively and at low cost compared to the benefits of eliminating the likelihood of accidental data loss or theft. This could be a manufacturer, law firm, medical facility, mortgage broker, or state or county agency. All should implement a data sanitization program at this level. They will also be contributing to their ESG goals by being able to account for carbon credits for any used devices that stay in the circular economy.

The most mature organizations use a similar process. They may handle extremely sensitive data that requires extreme measures. The Defense Industrial Base (DIB), large hospitals, the Pentagon, and large banks need extra levels of assurance that they are truly destroying all data that leaves their control. They often forgo clawing back residual value in used laptops and computers by requiring physical destruction. Anecdotally, the NSA degausses every device with data on it before shipping them to a single service provider for shredding. For modern storage on SSDs, they shred them immediately. Many data centers have SLAs that bar them from allowing storage devices to leave their premises. They too degauss or shred devices in their facilities.

On the spectrum between small organizations and large organizations with highly sensitive data lies the vast majority with a large volume of turnover. These organizations include an IT asset disposition provider in their process.

An ITAD will provide data sanitization on every device they receive. It is up to the organization how they select and then manage the ITAD relationship. The most important decision is when to sanitize the device. The options are as follows:

- As soon as the device is turned in to the IT department. Commercial software (not DBAN) can be used to perform the operation.

- When the devices are processed for delivery to the ITAD. So, a batch operation is performed whenever enough devices are collected such as weekly, monthly, or annually.

- When the device is picked up by the ITAD. Some ITADs will perform the data sanitization in your facilities before they are put on their trucks.

- In the ITAD's facility. The ITAD will take steps to ensure they keep the devices secure during transport. They provide a record of receipt when the devices reach their facility.

To determine the process you are going to use, it helps to be paranoid. Can you trust any third party to physically protect your devices during transport? Would a bad actor, like a spy agency, competitor, or data thief, target the transport vehicles? Would they bribe the driver? Some ITADs have vehicles that lock the driver out of the rear compartment and have an SLA that requires the driver to go directly from your loading dock to the ITAD facility. Savvy customers have included GPS tracking devices disguised as hard drives in their shipments. They report that all too often the drivers make multiple stops at gas stations, fast-food restaurants, and other customers, on their trips.

To understand what happens to your devices in an ITAD facility, see Chapter 8, "Asset Disposition," section 8.2 ITAD Operations.

## 7.3   Servers and Network Gear

Network gear also has critical data on it. Many appliances have hard drive or SSD storage. Security appliances need to store software revisions and a constant stream of updated signatures sent from the manufacturer. They may also have backup images on them to restore the devices to a previous state. They also store logs of every connection that passes through them. Every employee behind a firewall has their browsing activity recorded in these logs. Every outside connection or attempt to connect is stored. Most important, many network devices contain management credentials stored in cleartext. On top of that, digital certificates may be stored in a device. All of this critical data is subject to loss or theft if the device leaves the owner's control.

Routers are network devices, usually hardware but often purely software running on a server or VM. They are configured with multiple physical ports. The router makes simple decisions based on routing tables stored in memory: in response to an incoming connection via one port, the router determines what port to send the connection out over. When a user wants to get to the Internet, for instance, the router determines that the requested destination IP address is meant for one of the four billion IP addresses on the Internet and sends the packets out the port connected to the ISP's router. The ISP's router makes the determination based on the destination IP address and which organization owns that IP address and forwards the packets on to the ISP that is responsible for that range of IP addresses.

The router may be managed through a graphical user interface but is often controlled by a command-line interface (CLI). A network engineer logs in either through a physical port or over the network to get console access. They can add fixed routes, network masks, and assign usernames and passwords to other managers. They can also install updates to the router's software and program access control lists (ACLs), which serve as a simple firewall. The administrator could, for instance, deny access for anyone attempting to connect to the data center over the port reserved for Telnet. If an attacker had the login credentials of a router they could reroute traffic in damaging ways or cause other harm. Access credentials are all too often shared among many users and reused for many devices. Thus, if a router was taken out of service and sold on eBay, an attacker could purchase it and extract information from it that would identify what network it was meant to manage and provide all of the credentials necessary for logging in remotely. If an organization does not change infrastructure passwords, often the attacker could log in and significantly disrupt network operations.

The best practice is to include routers in an information lifecycle policy and schedule them for data sanitization before they are disposed of.

Firewalls are similar to routers but have more granular controls on network connections. Rules can be added to a firewall policy based on more than the source/destination/port or protocol. These rules can include user or group identity, time of day, and even geolocation data (no traffic allowed from China, for instance). Firewalls, like routers, can be subverted to allow an attacker in. They are more likely to have spinning disk or solid-state memory for backup images and storing logs. Firewalls should be completely sanitized as they are decommissioned.

Unified threat management (UTM) devices are extensions of firewalls created by adding new features. The most universal feature is to add block lists based on URLs to control where an employee can go on the Internet. These lists, arranged by categories such as pornography, hate sites, streaming services, etc., can be invoked based on an employee's role. For instance, you may want to restrict people in general from going to job boards from their work computers, but the HR department may need access to those job boards for posting job openings.

UTM devices also offer enhanced network defenses like signature-based intrusion prevention, blocking outward-bound command-and-control messages from bot-infected devices, or even full antivirus inspection. These appliances should never be allowed to leave an organization's control without being completely wiped.

Software-defined wide area networking (SDWAN) devices are the modern-day router. They are merely routers that can run applications. They usually have more storage than a router. All of the onboard memory, including the storage, should be completely wiped before disposal.

## 7.3.1 Edge Computing

The cloud has given rise to a new layer of computing, the edge. Although the cloud is envisioned as amorphous and disbursed, it is actually standardized and centralized in the data centers of various cloud providers like Amazon AWS, Google Cloud Platform, and Microsoft Azure. Centralization leads to bottlenecks and long paths for packets to traverse as they make their way from a user device, through the corporate network, to a series of ISPs, onto a backbone, and finally to the cloud provider's data center where it is finally routed to the virtual machine or container that is providing the requested service.

The "edge" that we interact with every day is content delivery networks. Providers like CloudFlare and Akamai host caching servers in hundreds of data centers around the world. In this way, the content on a single web server or application server is replicated all over the world to minimize the transit time to the content as well as dramatically expand the ability to serve content to millions of users. Think of this edge as the cloud edge.

Another "edge" is the equipment maintained by telecom service providers in their central offices. The central office (CO) used to be where all the copper lines from telephones were terminated and the traffic dumped onto the telecom backbone. Today, the edge is where all traffic from wireless connections is routed for processing before it is handed off to rival carriers or dumped onto the Internet. Telecom providers seek to offer additional processing on data that flows through their edge, at additional service fees.

Of course, CDNs and telecom providers have their own data sanitization requirements for decommissioned network gear, but the edge that poses a data sanitization issue for manufacturers, distribution warehouses, and transportation providers is the one provisioned and used for their own data processing.

Cloud computing and storage are expensive. Therefore, organizations that generate and process a lot of data want to minimize the data that is pushed to the cloud. They can do this by preprocessing that data as close to its original as possible. Imagine hundreds of sensors in an oil and gas refinery. Most of the sensors are reporting nominal conditions most of the time. The only data of value is data that indicates a change. So, sensor data can be fed into an edge computer where it is deduplicated and compressed.

A series of security cameras deployed throughout a large complex like a public arena, or even an entire city, streams continuous feeds to an edge computer that displays each camera's output on a screen for the security watchers. Imagine the amount of storage required to record a stairwell 24 hours a day. The edge computer could be programmed to store only footage when there is movement in the stairwell. All the important data would be recorded and time-stamped. None of the millions of restatic frames would be stored.

In section 7.5, we discuss IoT devices and the data that may reside on them. The new realm of edge computing means there will be larger devices that collect and store all of the data from these devices. Smart city proposals include cameras and sensors for monitoring automobile, bicycle, scooter, and pedestrian traffic. This form of edge computing may also make independent decisions to control traffic lights or signage. Power, gas, and water meters on every home record and control essential services. Edge computing servers in neighborhoods may be accessible to vandals and thieves.

As edge computing takes off, it will lead to a new generation of devices, often in industrial form factors, hardened against extreme environments, or made tamper proof. These edge computing devices may not have the aftermarket appeal of high volumes of expensive laptops. So, disposing of them may be problematic. It is important to identify early what data resides on these devices and incorporate it into a data sanitization program from the start.

The proliferation of devices in a digital world is inevitable. Edge computing poses a problem because it may be decades before ITAD operations are built to handle the responsible recycling of devices for which there is not a viable aftermarket. Unlike office equipment, each organization may have to incorporate data sanitization capabilities designed for their specialized equipment.

## 7.4  Mobile Devices

As mobile devices have supplanted laptops and PCs as the dominant market for computing devices, the issue of data sanitization of these devices has come to the forefront. While Android devices have the largest market share, IOS devices have the highest resale value.

Those that question the wisdom of Apple's lack of entry level iPhones in its product mix would be well served to remember Alfred Sloan's product strategy. Sloan was president of General Motors from 1923 to 1937 and chairman of the board from 1937 to 1956. Using a management concept dubbed *centralized decentralization*, Sloan created a product mix to cover the lifetime of a consumer: a Chevrolet for a first-time buyer, a Pontiac for a sporty second car, an Oldsmobile for the middle aged, and a Cadillac for an older financially established generation. When questioned about the low-end entry level, he pointed out that was what the used car market addressed.

There is no question that the entry level for iPhones is used iPhones. Millions of iPhones are passed on to children every year as their parents upgrade their phones. On top of that, exchange programs managed by Apple and telecom companies add millions of devices to the used cell phone market.

There is a healthy and vibrant market for used cell phones, from outdated Motorola flip phones to the top-of-the-line Samsung and Apple products. Wander the back aisles of the Mobile World Congress held each year in Barcelona and you will witness a buzz among the booths of resellers, refurbishers, accessory vendors, ITADS, and middlemen. Deals are made on the show floor that determine the movement of millions of devices around the world as they are collected and resold between multiple parties before re-entering the market as consumer devices.

## 7.4.1  Crypto-Erase

Most mobile phones have incorporated encryption for all data that resides on them. Apple led the way, and Android followed suit.

Mobile devices are secured with encryption algorithms and keys that are strong enough to prevent decryption even by the most capable intelligence agencies. This has been a benefit to the cause of data sanitization. If you attach an Android or IOS device to a forensic capture and analysis tool, all you would see is random ones and zeros, impossible to decipher without the encryption key. Those keys are stored on the device in a secure enclave and unlocked only when the owner enters their PIN. All a processor has to do is make all of the data on a device unrecoverable and destroy those keys. A 128 GB iPhone can be effectively erased in seconds instead of the hours needed to overwrite memory.

The process of rendering a memory store unreadable by key destruction is called *crypto-erase*. But don't forget the difference between *erase* and *sanitization*. Data sanitization requires that the process used, be it shredding, overwriting, or crypto-erasure, is verified and documented. On a cell phone, this means attempting to recover the encryption keys from the area in memory in which they are stored and to certify that the operation was successful. The rest of memory should also be sampled to verify the data is unrecoverable.

## 7.4.2  Mobile Phone Processing

Most ITADs are more than happy to process cell phones because the residual value can be much higher than for a five-year-old laptop. Notebook PCs surged from 173 to 220 million shipments at the onset of COVID-19 but are leveling out at 260 million a year, whereas cell phone sales are five times higher at 1.4 billion a year.

Some companies specialize in processing cell phones. Often they are not R2 certified because they do not contract directly with enterprises. Rather, they collect used cell phones from drop boxes, charities, and cell phone stores. They invariably provide data erasure because it is required to prepare a phone for resale, but they are less likely to document that erasure has occurred.

An ITAD's facilities for processing cell phones is similar to that for other device processing but is usually separate from the lines that process laptops and PCs. They may just sort the phones and grade them for resale to a specialist facility. Or they have all of their own operations that can sanitize, clean, repair screens, or disassemble for parts. Cell phone processors have to take extraordinary measures to prevent theft by their own employees because a used iPhone could have a street value of $600 or more.

### 7.4.3    Enterprise Data Erasure for Mobile Devices

Enterprises have two approaches to mobile devices: bring your own device (BYOD) and issuing corporate-owned devices.

#### 7.4.3.1    Bring Your Own Device

BYOD is the most common practice. An employer allows each employee to use their own smart phone for interacting with corporate data. The employee is issued credentials for accessing corporate email and applications. They may require the employee to download and install additional management software to allow the IT department to control credentials, monitor location, and revoke access if the phone is lost or stolen. They can also enforce policies to require that a PIN or biometrics be used to unlock the phone. A mobile device management (MDM) solution is used to provide all of these functions. In addition to managing the corporate apps, an MDM solution should be used to wipe any corporate data that may reside on a phone when it is reported lost or stolen or when the employee leaves the organization. Data tools can be used to scan the devices for PII and other critical data assets.

#### 7.4.3.2    Corporate-Issued Devices

The alternative to BYOD is for the organization to purchase, configure, and control standard-issue mobile devices. This gives them the ability to enforce policies that otherwise might be considered an invasion of the employee's privacy. It ensures that all devices can be managed and configured and can reduce the burden on the IT department for troubleshooting remote access issues.

# 7.5 Internet of Things: Unconventional Computing Devices

Any data sanitization program should take into account the ongoing revolution in the Internet of Things—those devices that do not fall into the categories of traditional computing devices like desktops, laptops, tablets, and phones.

It is estimated that IoT comprises 13 billion devices today, projected to grow to 30 billion by 2030. A data sanitization program should identify which devices are deployed in the enterprise and what kind of data they may have on them. The secure data lifecycle should look further into where the data generated by these devices resides. Does it leave the control of the enterprise? Is it captured and stored by a third party?

The category of devices that may have to be identified, tracked, and eventually sanitized includes the following.

## 7.5.1 Printers and Scanners

These devices often have onboard memory that spools data sent to a printer or created by a document scanner. In addition, they are often connected to the corporate network, making them susceptible to network-based attacks that may seek to steal the data that resides in their memory. In addition, when a printer is discarded, a process should be in place to ensure the data is sanitized.

One scenario that is rarely considered is that printers and scanners are a way for data to cross security zones. Imagine that the printer in the CFO's office is moved to the IT department (because the IT department gets the cast-offs). Sensitive documents such as financials, or those related to M&A, may be in the printer's memory, and now the printer is being used by technically savvy IT personnel who may be curious about the content of the printer's memory.

## 7.5.2 Landline Phones

The modern desk phone is a network-attached device. It may contain a directory of phone numbers stored in speed dial, or a list of recent numbers called and the time and duration of each call. It could have stored PINs for conference rooms or retrieving voicemail.

## 7.5.3 Industrial Control Systems

ICS devices include management workstations, programmable logic controllers (PLCs), and sensors and actuators. A very sophisticated attacker may attempt to get access to these devices to understand how best to attack the systems they control. Leaving these devices open to the Internet or not sanitizing them when they are disposed of could lead to major disruptions.

### 7.5.4   HVAC Controls

Sensors and control systems for building environments can yield valuable data. An attacker who had access to any stored data could determine when the building is in use or attempt to modify building controls to disrupt operations.

### 7.5.5   Medical Devices

In a hospital or clinic there are many systems that record data that may be considered sensitive. A simple heart rate monitor or wearable EKG sensor can reveal the status of a patient's health, data that should be secured and, when not needed, sanitized. When the devices are disposed of, they should be directed to an ITAD for processing. The high-end devices that are usually versions of PCs and laptops should be completely sanitized. Smaller devices like sensors should be scheduled for destruction if they cannot be erased, especially if the data on them can be associated with a patient.

   This list helps highlight that data is everywhere. A data sanitizing program must find, identify, and classify every place that data may reside before it can be tracked throughout its lifecycle. Data sanitization is the last phase, and it requires the devices on which data resides be effectively erased or destroyed. Now let's address one of the most complicated IoT devices, automobiles.

## 7.6   Automobiles

Automobiles are a special case of the Internet of Things. After 100 years of design evolution, cars, trucks, and buses have entered the digital age. Every vehicle has hundreds of onboard microprocessors for fuel control, brakes, power steering (drive by wire), and human comfort. Air bag sensors distributed to strategic locations inform a brain that has to decide when to fire the explosive charges in the critical milliseconds when they can protect an occupant's life.

   Autonomous vehicles resemble computer systems on wheels with multiple redundant processors making millions of decisions a second and communicating with the cloud to tap into machine learning algorithms that learn how to avoid collisions, read traffic signs, and monitor all the other vehicles nearby. Tesla's latest vehicles have more than 100 million lines of code in onboard systems.

   But let's start with vehicle onboard entertainment systems; they are simple and decoupled from the actual operation of the vehicle.

Most new cars have entertainment systems to control radio channels and video programming displays for the passengers (we like to think the driver is not watching videos). These systems also accommodate hands-free driving by pairing with an occupant's cell phone to make and receive calls. Pairing with mobile devices raises an issue in two use cases.

The most concerning issue is rental vehicles. In the United States there were 2.2 million vehicles in the rental car agencies' fleets accounting for millions of returns a month. Any occupant in a rental vehicle may pair their cell phone with the infotainment system. That pairing can take different forms. One is that the infotainment system effectively mirrors the screen on the user's phone. This is less problematic than the other way.

The potentially harmful way of pairing means that a lot of data is passed from the phone to the infotainment system. This includes playlists for audio files, complete contacts, images associated with those contacts, and even call and text history. It is trivial for any of the subsequent passengers of that rental vehicle to recall this information.

To stress the risk of this information being exposed, consider a couple of scenarios.

A celebrity movie star rents a vehicle at the Hollywood Burbank airport for their trip to Hollywood. They use the infotainment system to sync with their cell phone so they do not get pulled over by the California Highway Patrol for breaking the hands-free law. The infotainment system captures the movie star's complete contact list and call records. The next person to rent the vehicle peruses the previous renter's information and collects the phone numbers of all the other celebrities that the movie star has ever talked to. There may even be text conversations retrieved that could be salacious or revealing of private relationships and business dealings.

An official from GCHQ visiting the National Security Agency (located a short drive from BWI) rents a car in Baltimore. The next renter may be from an unfriendly spy agency or a journalist. They plug in a tool that captures not only the previous information synced by the GCHQ person but every phone ever synced and stored on the onboard hard drive.

These two use cases, if exploited, would cause a furor and lead to rental agencies taking steps to avoid these incidents in the future. But in the EU, subject to GDPR, the use case of any data subject renting a car would require an auditable process to erase the stored memory of every vehicle each time it is returned.

## 7.6.1   Off-Lease Vehicles

Lease returns are of particular interest because in most cases vehicles being returned after their leases expire are two to three years old and therefore probably equipped with modern infotainment systems. They may have been paired and synced with several phones belonging to family members and friends. Other data that may be recoverable is trip reports from onboard navigation systems. Certainly the owner's "home" address is probably recorded as a frequent destination.

Dealerships and manufacturers have established processes in place to receive lease returns. They are cleaned, repaired, and often spruced up with new paint, in preparation for being sold back into the market as used vehicles. These processes should be enhanced by adding a data sanitization procedure.

Data should be erased from lease return vehicles as soon as they are returned. It should be the first step when an owner turns in their keys. A record of the sanitization should be kept with the vehicle paperwork throughout its entire life. Perhaps a central database of erasure records should be kept by vehicle identity number (VIN) so anyone selling a car can check to see if it has been properly sanitized.

## 7.6.2   Used Vehicle Market

Throughout a vehicle's life, it changes ownership several times. While many vehicles pass through the hands of dealerships, many of them are sold directly from owner to owner. In that case, the responsibility for removing access to data may reside with the selling party. At a minimum, they should unpair their devices, a function that is easily accessible on the onboard menus of the infotainment system. A similar delete function should be available in the onboard navigation system.

## 7.6.3   Sanitization of Automobiles

As of this writing, the authors know of no efforts to create a standard process to sanitize the data in vehicles. Large leasing companies and resellers of vehicles should be aware that they may fall under the purview of data privacy regulations, especially GDPR. To get ahead of the regulators and to avoid potential legal issues, these organizations should add data sanitization processes to their vehicle-handling playbooks.

The processes should be put in place for whenever a vehicle changes ownership. At the very least, the onboard control panel should be accessed, and any paired cell phones should be unpaired. This makes the data inaccessible from the infotainment system menus. Yet, as with a PC, just because the file system cannot see data, there is no assurance that the onboard storage medium (a spinning hard drive in older systems, solid-state memory in modern systems) is not subject to forensic analysis.

It is possible to access the data stored in an infotainment system through the on-board diagnostics (OBD) port or the USB port. A small thumb drive with an adapter could be plugged into these ports to extract all the data stored.

Those ports could also be used to access the data for overwriting. A process that included inserting such a device could easily be added to the change of control processes for vehicles. It should be done soon after a vehicle is returned from rental, or lease, or when it is handed over after sale to a dealer or reseller.

## 7.7   Summary

By now you will agree that keeping track of all these different types of data-ridden devices is a problem. As long as a device is in the control of the data owner, it only represents a potential problem thanks to the threat of loss or theft. But at the end of a device's useful life, the data problem rises to the top. How do you ensure that that data is eradicated before the device changes hands? In the next chapter, we introduce you to the IT asset disposition industry.

CHAPTER

# 8

# Asset Disposition

The PC revolution, born in the late 1980s, gave rise to desktop computing in the enterprise. Every so-called knowledge worker became empowered to create and use data from their own desktop. Over time the only employees not equipped with their own computers were those that did not have desks: line workers on the shop floor, security guards walking their beats, food service people in the kitchen, or serving patrons. Following Moore's law, computers doubled in capacity every 18 months as CPUs became faster, storage became cheaper, and capacity increased. This leads to a refresh cycle of two to three years for corporations. Even government agencies have to invest in upgraded PCs, although not as frequently as commercial enterprises.

The digital era, ushered in by personal computing and fueled by the advent of the Internet, is characterized by continuous growth in computing power and volume of data. In return, the world economy saw increases in productivity and economic growth. One aspect of this growth was a rapid rise in out-of-date computing devices as new models made previous models completely obsolete. This is a pattern that is continuing to this day, and it means that millions of PCs, laptops, and tablets are scheduled for disposal every year.

It did not take long to recognize that PCs and CRTs should not end up in landfills. One of the initial drivers was that printed circuit boards and other components contained trace amounts of gold, silver, palladium, and other precious metals. Recycling centers would pay for old computers. For the most part, they would remove the components that contained the valuable metals and recover those metals via smelting. The rest of the materials, many that contained toxic chemicals, like arsenic, would end up in landfills.

As the impact on the environment of all of this waste was realized, countries began to regulate computer disposal. Besides, last year's models were often still usable. They could be repurposed for classrooms or sold in the aftermarket to home users who could not afford the latest and greatest computers. A home could be found for them in less-developed countries.

With reuse, a data security concern arose. The new owners of computers and storage devices may discover old data on them that could compromise the original owner. In a modern-day equivalent of dumpster divers, researchers and cybercriminals may purchase used computers and hard drives to inspect them for valuable data.

Out of recycling and refurbishing arose the modern-day IT asset disposition industry. Thousands of facilities in mostly developed countries receive millions of devices a day. In addition to following protocols for the safe disposal of waste, they have introduced strict procedures for ensuring that a customer's data is sanitized before a machine or hard drive is reused.

## 8.1   Contracting and Managing Your ITAD

When you create your data sanitization program, somewhere at the bottom, it will probably have a requirement to hand off devices to an ITAD. Even those organizations that decide to "go it alone" when it comes to fixing, cleaning, and reselling used devices will have devices for which there are no buyers on eBay, or they are beyond repair. In either case, they have to be disposed of, and placing them in a trash receptacle behind the building is environmentally irresponsible.

Choosing an ITAD to work with depends on several factors. The proximity of an ITAD's facility will drive both cost and provenance factors. Shipping crates of discarded PCs and laptops incur a per-mile charge. Long-distance shipping means the device is exposed to loss or theft at every waypoint on the route to the recycling center.

The cost of working with an ITAD can be offset dramatically by residual value in the devices being discarded. A one-year-old, high-end laptop computer can command a good price in the aftermarket. Most ITADs will take your devices on consignment and share the residual value with you. Alternatively, they may purchase them outright from you.

While costs are a top concern, data governance should be a top priority when selecting an ITAD. Things to consider include the following:

**Asset tracking** Does the ITAD take accurate inventory at your shipping dock? Do they tag each device with their own tracking labels and provide you with the data to cross-correlate your asset identifier with their tracking system? Do they have a system you can access that shows the status of each asset as it is received at their facility, sanitized, processed, and ultimately resold, parted out, or disposed of?

**Data sanitization** Does the ITAD use a systematic tool for data sanitization? Can they accommodate your requirements for the number and type of overwrite passes as defined in your information lifecycle policy?

**Attestation** Does the ITAD provide an immutable (digitally signed) record of sanitization that is tied to the asset identifier?

**Software license recovery** Before sanitizing a PC, does the ITAD perform a software license discovery scan? This is another opportunity to recover value from discarded devices that may be assigned a license for expensive software from Microsoft, Adobe, or any number of enterprise software providers. Those licenses can be reassigned to machines that are still in use.

**Certifications** Does the ITAD have a current certification from an industry standards body (R2, e-Steward, or NAID)? When was the last certification? Do they provide the report of the most recent audit? Does it call out any deficiencies that need to be addressed?

## 8.2  ITAD Operations

An ITAD usually employs hundreds of people in a processing facility. If you visit an ITAD, you will most likely see a large warehouse physically separated into different processing areas. An ITAD is organized to ensure minimum exposure of your data before it is sanitized. At the receiving dock, devices are separated into different pallets or containers depending on the process flow they are scheduled for: refurbishment, parting out, or destruction and disposal.

Every device is assigned a tag, or the tags that were assigned when the devices were picked up at your facility are recorded. Each container is further identified with a label that identifies it to the plant personnel. They can scan the label to check the whole batch into their processing area and again when they pass it off to the next stage.

The very first step in processing is the power-on check. Can the device be powered up so that data can be sanitized? Imagine the number of power cords an ITAD has to have on hand to be able to accommodate the hundreds of connectors, and consider the power requirements. If the device cannot be powered up, it must be further processed to see if a new battery or other repair can fix it. If not, can the hard drive be removed and accessed for sanitization and eventual sale or recycling? If the device is unrepairable, it may be scheduled for its constituent components to be disassembled for reuse in other devices to be repaired. A screen may be used to replace a cracked screen on another laptop, for instance. Or the RAM chips could be used in another laptop.

If a computer can be powered up, the next step is license recovery. If requested by the customer, the computer is scanned for software license keys, which are recorded and reported to the customer so they can reuse them.

The next step is data sanitization. ITADs have long stations where dozens of computers can be simultaneously sanitized. To completely sanitize a device, it must be provided power, connected to a network, and booted from a remote system. Every disk sector, including boot sectors, is going to be overwritten, so the onboard operating system will be of no use.

It can take hours to effectively overwrite a modern hard drive with hundreds of gigabytes or several terabytes of disk space. As the devices are being overwritten, they display a large progress tracker on their screen. In this way, the operators in the data sanitization department can easily monitor progress with a quick glance at the rows of machines.

When the overwriting process is complete, so is the data governance burden. The data is irretrievably erased. A record of sanitization is created and tied to the asset identifiers so the customer can verify data sanitization for any machine they decommissioned and sent to the ITAD. An audit of your data sanitization program will check periodically to see if machines taken out of use have indeed been sanitized.

From this stage on, an ITAD focuses on extracting the most value from each device. It is graded and assigned to different processing areas for cleaning and refurbishing, repair, disassembly, or shredding if it has no value.

Glass in CRT and laptop screens is processed separately. It may have to be cleaned of environmentally harmful substances like phosphorus. It can be pulverized and prepared for shipping to separate facilities for use as an additive to enamel paints, or it may be mixed with asphalt for paving. If harmful material cannot be removed, then it is melted and poured into molds. In the form of glass blocks, it can be sent to a landfill where it would take millions of years for any environmental harm to occur.

The ITAD is responsible for the safe disposal of all the material it handles. Ideally the recyclers it sends material to are also certified to handle and dispose of the glass, plastic, and metal in a safe and responsible manner.

Note that this chapter has been focused on laptops and PCs. There are many more devices that contain data. Each of them poses challenges. Often they are processed by the same ITAD facilities. In the next chapters, we address cell phones, IoT, and network gear.

## 8.3 Sustainability and Green Tech

ITADs are an important contributor to sustainability. By taking in old electronic equipment and refurbishing it for reuse, they are extending the life of devices and creating a supply of lower-cost products. If a device cannot be restored to its original function, the ITAD can disassemble it to save the component parts for repairing other devices. Finally, any material that cannot be reused is separated and responsibly recycled.

## 8.4 Contribution from R2

The Responsible Recycling (R2) standard is maintained by Sustainable Electronics Recycling International (SERI). SERI is a nonprofit organization that follows ANSI standards for establishing and maintaining R2. A Technical Advisory Committee (TAC) meets regularly by conference call and annually in person. The TAC consists of industry participants, including consultants, R2 auditors, and people with extensive ITAD experience. As of November 2020, there were 939 recycling facilities worldwide that were certified to the R2 2013 standard.

The R2 Standard was first published in a 2008 version, and the first two facilities were certified by 2010. It was updated in 2013, 2018, and 2020. A plan is in place to transition the 2013 certification to the new standard R2v3 by July 1, 2023.

For data sanitization, the relevant articles are "R2v3 Article 7: Data Security" and "R2v3 Appendix B – Data Sanitization" in *The Sustainable Electronics Reuse & Recycling (R2) Standard* by SERI (2020).

### 8.4.1 Tracking Throughput

General principle: To track and manage the throughput of all electronic equipment, components, and materials, and maintain sufficient records to document the flow.

This section provides auditability and assurance that your equipment is handled appropriately as it is processed in an R2 certified facility.

### 8.4.2    Data Security

General principle: To provide for the security and sanitization of all data storage devices as appropriate to the type of device and level of sensitivity of the data.

The complete R2v3, Article 7, is available at `https://sustainableelectron ics.org/welcome-to-r2v3` along with Appendix B, "Data Sanitization," in *The Sustainable Electronics Reuse & Recycling (R2) Standard* by SERI (2020). As the only standard for data sanitization that incorporates the process, it is a valuable guide that could form the basis of an internal data sanitization program.

The R2 standard was created by a group that had direct experience in ITAD operations. Not only does it require that processing facilities have a data sanitization plan, but it requires they have security controls in place, including physical separation of devices that still contain a customer's data and strict access controls. Most ITADs have well-established controls on employee and visitor access. To enter the facility, you must either leave your phone outside or register it before passing through a metal detector. Keep in mind that these facilities process millions of dollars of equipment every day. They have to have measures in place to prevent anyone from walking off with iPhones and high-end laptops. Ask them about disaster preparedness. How do they prevent loss during a fire drill, for instance?

Also note section 7.1.E, "Potential associations to network services." Cell phones, if they still have their SIM cards in place or if they can establish a Wi-Fi connection, can make a network connection and restore all the data that was just removed from them!

## 8.5    e-Stewards Standard for Responsible Recycling and Reuse of Electronic Equipment

The e-Stewards initiative began in 2003 with a group of more than 40 electronic waste recyclers in the United States and Canada that pledged to use globally responsible, safe means to process electronic waste. The focus was on reducing toxic waste. Working with the Basel Action Network, they sought to create a standard for recycling waste. In 2006 they began to work with the EPA funded Responsible Recycling (R2) group but disagreed with the way the R2 standard treated the export of toxic waste to developing countries. They split from R2 to create the "e-Stewards Standard," which has much more stringent controls on the export of toxic materials. The *e-Stewards Standard for Responsible Recycling and Reuse of Electronic Equipment* was published in 2009.

An ITAD that is certified to the e-Stewards Standard is audited and accountable for the downstream disposition of waste.

The latest version of the *e-Stewards Standard* (v4.1) was published on February 22, 2022, and all certified organizations have to follow the new version by April 22, 2023.

Data sanitization is covered in Appendix 8.9.3, which requires all devices to be sanitized to either the latest national standard published in a country or region or the latest version of NIST SP 800-88, whichever is more stringent.

Unlike the R2 Standard, e-Stewards continues to point to national data standards and does not go into as much detail.

Appendix 8.9.4 calls for the verification of data destruction for all devices whether by logical erasure or physical destruction. It requires a record to be kept of the procedures used to enact that destruction.

## 8.6   i-SIGMA

The National Association for Information Destruction (NAID) was formed in 1995 and merged into another standards body, PRISM, in 2018 to form the International Secure Information Governance & Management Association. I-SIGMA claims more than 2,000 secure destruction and records and information management service providers as members. NAID created and maintains the NAID AAA Certification, which is widely used by ITADs and independent data destruction service firms.

For an organization to be certified, they must be in compliance with the NAID standard and be re-certified every year to ensure continued compliance.

Unlike R2 or e-Stewards, the NAID certification is focused on ITAD operations. For instance, it has sections on the proper controls used for vehicles that transport devices from a customer to the recycling facility. It also covers data sanitization in mobile stations or customer sites.

During an audit, the facility must provide two hard drives and SSDs that have been erased, and the auditor sends them to a lab for verification. If the data has not been sanitized, the facility does not receive a NAID certification. The auditor can show up unannounced at a facility as a further measure to ensure that facilities stay in compliance.

Without specifying exact methods of overwriting, the standard requires that there be a written and verifiable process for the overwriting of hard drives and/or solid-state memory circuits (devices). There are similar documentation requirements for paper and magnetic tape and the degaussing of hard drives.

## 8.7   FACTA

There is a U.S. regulation called the Fair and Accurate Credit Transactions Act of 2003 (FACTA) that has language covering the destruction of "consumer reports." The FTC website explains that the rule applies to anyone that uses consumer reports, which means: consumer reporting companies; lenders; insurers; employers; landlords; government agencies; mortgage brokers and car dealers;

attorneys; private investigators; debt collectors; individuals who pull consumer reports on prospective home employees, such as nannies or contractors; and entities that maintain information in consumer reports as part of their role as a service provider to other organizations covered by the rule.

FACTA required several government agencies to adopt comparable and consistent rules regarding the disposal of sensitive consumer report information. These are the FTC, the Federal Reserve Board, the Office of the Comptroller of the Currency, the Federal Deposit Insurance Corporation, the Office of Thrift Supervision, the National Credit Union Administration, and the Securities and Exchange Commission.

The FTC put into force their rules for data destruction in 2005. The Disposal Rule requires disposal practices that are "reasonable and appropriate" to prevent the unauthorized access to—or use of—information in a consumer report. It offers as guidance these requirements:

- Burn, pulverize, or shred papers containing consumer report information so that the information cannot be read or reconstructed.

- Destroy or erase electronic files or media containing consumer report information so that the information cannot be read or reconstructed.

- Conduct due diligence and hire a document destruction contractor to dispose of material specifically identified as consumer report information consistent with the rule.

Due diligence could include the following:

- Reviewing an independent audit of a disposal company's operations and/ or its compliance with the rule

- Obtaining information about the disposal company from several references

- Requiring that the disposal company be certified by a recognized trade association

- Reviewing and evaluating the disposal company's information security policies or procedures

Most organizations that classify personal information separately and have a policy for data sanitization of such will be able to comply with these requirements. e-Stewards, R2, and NAID certified ITADS will suffice for the last points.

But FACTA and the various agency requirements for data disposal broaden the universe of people and organizations that have to follow a data sanitization procedure. Does the used car lot that pulls your credit report shred the printouts and erase the digital records they pull?

Data sanitization is becoming a widespread requirement of regulators. This should be taken into account in any data governance program. Make sure you have a data sanitization policy as part of your overall data lifecycle management plan.

## 8.8 Summary

ITADs play an important role in the circular economy. Advancing technology has become part of society, government, and industry. The benefits are many: better crop yields, cleaner water, better medicines including vaccines that can be developed in months instead of years. But technology and the drive to upgrade is creating an environmental problem. On the consumption and logistics side, we have vast amounts of natural resources from oil for energy and materials to rare earths and metals that go into modern computers and smartphones. ITADs provide the critical services to reclaim some of those materials while repurposing the millions of useful devices that have already been manufactured.

In the next chapter, we hear from three pioneers of the IT asset disposition industry, each in a different region and each with different paths. All of them have recognized the importance of what they do for sustainability. They may have started out reclaiming gold and silver from printed circuit boards, but as the value of used devices became apparent, they moved into restoring and reselling devices. Now they are playing a part in the move to a circular economy and sustainability.

# Stories from the Field

The following three stories from Europe, Australia, and the United States are told by executives from 3stepIT, TES – IT Lifecycle Solutions, and Ingram Micro. Each of them followed a different journey to sustainability and the circular economy.

Carmen Ene tells how she was recruited away from IBM to lead 3stepIT–a Nordic leader in Technology Lifecycle Management–and quickly grew the business throughout Europe by partnering with global financial institutions that offer leasing for technology assets. 3stepIT has over 25 years of experience in supporting customers throughout all phases of an asset's lifecycle: from acquisition to management to giving it a second life through refurbishing.

Stuart Hebron relates the story of how he and Gary Steele grew with the industry from its beginnings when electronic recycling was all about recovering valuable metals and material from outdated equipment to today's reuse, refurbishment, and data protection required for the circular economy.

Todd Segers leads ITAD & Reverse Logistics operations for Ingram Micro, one of the largest computer technology distributors in the world. He shares his story of founding Green Asset Disposal in 2003, merging it with CloudBlue, and then being acquired by Ingram Micro.

In sum, these ITAD leaders paint a picture of an evolving market for services that sustain the ever-growing demand for newer technology. All the mega-trends in information technology, including advanced storage solutions, cloud transformation, data lakes required for AI and machine learning, IoT, and smartphones, drive demand for faster refresh cycles. Without the services of these three companies—and the thousands of smaller organizations—the world would suffer from a glut of waste going to landfills and polluting the air and water.

Modern ITADs promote sustainability by recovering value from used electronic devices, first by refurbishing and reselling them to other users and second by responsibly recycling the unusable devices to extract what parts and materials that are still useful and then ensuring that the remains are disposed of properly.

As regulations in Europe and the rest of the world go into effect, they are imposing requirements on organizations to support the "right to repair," reduce carbon footprints, and protect data privacy. Data sanitization plays an important role in achieving compliance with all of these items.

If devices are to be repaired by third parties, they must be sanitized of all data before they are processed. Data sanitization is the first step before diagnosis, evaluation, and ultimately fitting into the repair cycle. Reducing an individual's or an organization's carbon footprint must include consideration for the manufactured goods they consume. If they can account for the carbon and energy requirements that go into producing a product that they are discarding, they can get "credit" for making sure the product is reused. Instead of a net negative carbon score, on top of the carbon calculation for the new product, they can use devices that stay in use in secondary markets to reduce their calculated carbon footprint.

The data sanitization industry was created to address the risk of private data being leaked on discarded hard drives. It has evolved dramatically over 25 years to its important role in the entire circular economy.

## 9.1    3stepIT

*Carmen Ene is the CEO of 3stepIT, the largest full-cycle asset management company in Europe. They have formed a joint venture with BNP Paribas to offer financing, leasing, and acquisition support. In March 2022 they also partnered with CaixiaBank in Spain to extend their offering. CaixaBank will provide its clients—corporate, mid-market, and public-sector organizations—with BNP Paribas 3step IT's technology lifecycle management services, which simplify the acquisition, management, and refresh of business technology. Based on the principles of the circular economy, this solution also supports organizations seeking to decarbonize their operations as part of the net zero transition.*

I'm Romanian, born and educated in Bucharest. I'm a graduate of cybernetics. Cybernetics, when I was young, was the buzzword of the day. Today it's artificial intelligence, cloud, and analytics. Back then it was cybernetics. It sparked a lifelong passion for technology and its ability to create change, accelerate business growth, and improve society.

One of the founding fathers of cybernetics is Romanian, Dr. Ştefan Odobleja. But he was not in the grace of the reigning communist party. Therefore, he spent most of his life in house arrest. That was enough motive for me to go in a direction that supported science at that point in time. After the 1989 revolution, I joined a group of five people to form one of the first private companies in Romania. We were a bit more stylish than an America startup: we didn't start in a garage (maybe because we didn't have a garage); we started in a hotel room.

I understood the value technology could deliver from the outset, so under the lead of a respected industry expert, Dr. Dan Roman, we established a service organization for IBM, selling IBM hardware and software locally, and providing services that supported the technology. In a couple of years, we became the biggest company in Romania, and the business was acquired by IBM, which is how I joined the company in my first overseas job.

I went to Vienna, which was the center of Central and Eastern Europe, Middle East, and Africa. I had 20 wonderful years with IBM in five countries, through five completely different jobs. At one point I was running IBM global financing for Europe. I gained an incredible perspective on the global technology market, its important influence and ability to enable growth, and the opportunities and threats posed by data. And, crucially, tech's huge environmental and social impact.

In 2015, after 20 years with IBM, when I was thinking, what's next? Should I stay, or should I go? I got a call from a headhunter asking for someone to run 3stepIT. I really liked the business model. I like it even today. The owners and shareholders wanted to grow exponentially, and they needed help.

They were very successful in the Nordics, but they were looking to expand internationally. I joined the company in 2015, and in 2019 we signed a joint venture with BNP Paribas to expand in the rest of Europe. They brought the clients and the credit and the funding, and 3stepIT brought the services and the IT platform.

In 1995, Gartner coined the term *total cost of ownership*, and 3stepIT was formed in 1997 to provide services throughout an asset's lifetime. This core concept was novel and evolved into what today is the circular economy.

In those days, even at IBM, we were financing big mainframes and software. Nobody was really thinking of financing or doing fleet management for PCs. But they started with this idea: what happens with a PC when companies don't need it anymore? From the very beginning, they had in mind that they would promise the customer to take the equipment back and help them repurpose it.

We call ourselves 3stepIT because our offer comes in three steps.

In the first step, we help customers acquire in an easy way the equipment and, our sweet spot, the smart devices (laptops, mobile phones, everything that comes in big numbers and needs to be managed). During the acquisition phase, we help with the financing of this equipment.

Step 2 is managing these volumes of small devices during the primary lifetime. We developed our own systems to do this. The various functionality in our system puts the control in our customers' hands.

Customers know exactly where the equipment is, how long it has been in use, and who is using it. At the end of its primary life, we start sending messages. They have to return the equipment, and we make this return and renewal very easy. We do everything for the customers because normally a lot of headache is with the return.

We take the equipment back and send it to our refurbishing centers. We refurbish it, and we delete the information in a secured way, which is a big, big part of the service that we provide. When we delete the information, we have reports that are issued automatically from our asset management system to the customer to confirm that the information has been safely deleted. And then we resell it.

The strength of our model is that we have the complete process. You don't have to deal with many companies with different processes. We have complete visibility into how many devices each customer will be recycling next week and next year, which gives the customer an advantage.

People know they can come to us and know how many computers they could buy from us in the future. We don't sell to countries that don't have very rigorous legislation in terms of e-waste. For instance, we have been selling to a company in Finland for many years that loads new software on devices and distributes them to schools.

So, we are very well established in the Nordics. Since we signed the joint venture in Europe, we launched in six countries including Italy. Just a few weeks ago I opened in Spain with another partnership with the biggest bank, CaixiaBank.

We have 2.3 million assets under management. Last year, we refurbished 530,000 devices for resale.

We provide a tool to our customers that allows them to calculate their carbon emissions savings from reuse and resale. We also report on the successful data sanitization of each device.

Are there regulations in place that are going to require this reporting or require companies to drive toward net zero emissions? That is such an interesting thing.

I strongly believe that circularity is going to work. There are two things that are happening at the same time, and they are contradictory, but in the end they push toward the same direction.

First is digitalization. Everybody had digital projects before the pandemic. Some projects were more successful than others. But this crisis has pushed digitalization to an unprecedented level because everybody needs to digitalize.

With digitalization comes more data. It's growing exponentially.

The second thing is the crisis in the supply chain. With China locked down, it is harder to purchase new equipment. This drives demand for refurbished devices.

The circular economy is growing thanks to these two trends, new legislative pressures around the right to repair, and even consumer pressure. At 3stepIT we plan to grow with it and help it along.

## 9.2  TES – IT Lifecycle Solutions

*Stuart Hebron is the group CIO at TES – IT Lifecycle Solutions. His career tracks the emergence of the electronic equipment repair and refurbishing industry. He shares the story of how he and Gary Steele, group CEO, got together two decades ago and now have leadership roles in one of the largest ITADs in the Asian region. TES is in the process of being acquired by a large environmental solutions company in Korea to further their goals of providing sustainability services throughout the world.*

I started in electronics repair in 1985. I didn't realize at that point that what I was getting involved in was really about extended life—in particular around mobile phones.

In the late '80s the cost of a mobile phone was extremely high. The life expectancy was well beyond the one-year warranties that were provided.

In the UK, you didn't have rights to have access to spare parts and circuit diagrams for self-repair, so it was a specialized business. A lot of the smaller repair businesses were consolidated around Europe as the business grew and as the technology became more commonplace.

I spent a few years in the repair environment. The business was successful because it wasn't tied to the big guns in the industry. We spent a lot of time doing mobile phone repair for older models. Businesses were surrendering them for upgrades, and in the meantime consumers were starting to get onboard with mobile phones becoming a part of normal life.

They were looking at cheaper options. So, secondhand phone sales were a really big part of the business. I didn't do the sales, but I provided the repairs and the testing of that equipment to put it back into the secondhand market. And that is strangely how I met Gary Steele, who is the current CEO of Tes-amm.

Gary was running a mobile phone business that focused on small business and a lot of the services that revolved around how to keep the phone going. How do we keep the costs down and so on? In those days, it wasn't really about sustainability from the perspective of the environment; it was really around sustainability in a financial context. Sustainability isn't only around environmental factors.

Sustainability is about many things; we'll go into that later. But during that process, the attention started to turn to computers, and Gary had a couple of customers in the business space around his mobile comms that were interested in getting on board with a more digitized workplace.

Gary asked me if I knew anything about this computer stuff. And strangely I did for many years. And he said we should do something. He had a really good customer who wanted to do a couple of hundred new machines.

So we dove into computers, but I stayed outside of Gary's business at that point, working as a contractor/advisor. Then my wife became his PA, and over the years they've worked together. We've been pretty tight for a long time.

Gary had started to forge some relationships with regard to insurance replacement. One of the biggest insurers in England at the time was providing tech replacement for damaged, lost, repaired, and stolen equipment.

We were building and provisioning equipment and installing networks. As a side effect of that, Gary found he had a full warehouse of faulty secondhand—written-off—inventories from insurance companies and businesses.

Sometimes it would be used for repair stock and spare parts, but it got a little bit out of control. The reality set in that there was actually quite a lot of value in what he was sitting on. One man's trash is another man's treasure.

What we were doing was not called *IT asset disposition* back then. Even the concept of sustainability was not associated with our business of supplying spare parts to refurbishers.

I left England in the late 90s and moved to Australia. After Gary came for a visit, we decided to launch Just RecycleIT (JRI). Recycling and sustainability became an important part of what we did in the new business: extended life, spare parts, provision reverse logistics, and services that went with that. And then we were invited to the large consumer electronics show in Sydney. We attended as a representative of Queensland government's small business initiative. This is where we met Tes-amm.

Tes-amm Australia was started by Alvin Paidasa as a recycler for precious metal recovery and summit materials management. But Alvin was interested in the reuse business, so he wanted to work with us.

The first big project with Tes-amm was a joint venture between Team and JRI with a big Victorian education mass rollout. Shortly after we entered into joint discussion around the ITAD business with Computer Sciences Corporation and Hewlett Packard financial services. (HP eventually acquired CSC.)

The two rather large contracts that came from those talks kickstarted ITAD development not only in Australia but also for the entire company. A lot of the practices and policies we introduced at that time are still in play today. We had to counter resistance from the traditional recycling culture of the business itself.

The success of those contracts led to Tes-amm merging JRI into its business. My role became operations and technology director. Gary came on as the director of sales and marketing.

Today, ITAD is the strongest pillar in our financial model. We have grown the business both organically and through acquisition.

I spent 10 years evangelizing the ITAD business both within Tes-amm Australia and in the larger Tes-amm Group. An important part of ITAD operations is ensuring that data is securely removed from devices before they are processed. We originally used Kroll for that but switched to Blancco. We felt they had put a lot of work into making a product from the ground up to serve the ITAD space.

Gary traveled a lot to the extended Tes-amm operations and became chief of sales, then CMO, COO, and now CEO. He's been instrumental in developing the business either through acquisition, merger, and organic growth.

Over time, I took on a bigger role, culminating in accepting the position of CIO for the group in the early months of 2020, just when COVID was impacting the business.

And now SK ecoplant, based in Korea, has acquired TES. They have long viewed the sustainable IT lifecycle market strategically as a means to help create a zero-waste, zero-pollution circular economy.

## 9.2.1   Scale of Operations

We service mostly large organizations from 40 locations in 20 countries. We provide a full-cycle sustainability solution. Acquire IT assets, deploy them, set them up, get them out, recycle as required, sanitize as required, and pass on to resellers. We also provide some interesting lease management things, like predictive valuations of assets.

We provide equipment purchase for stock and hold it on behalf of customers as well as the financing required.

Refresh cycles for our customers vary. Aggressive adapters tend to want the latest and greatest equipment, but the norm is around three years, usually aligned to manufacturer warranty periods.

Supply issues during COVID have led to longer retention, but there are signs that organizations are doing a brisk cycle of upgrades now that we are on the backside of the slowdown.

I think we'll start to see that some of the attitudes toward asset life will change. We certainly saw an increase in secondhand acquisition of decent-quality assets in the e-tail space that were being acquired by businesses, in some cases big names, because they could not get access to what they wanted.

This may be a catalyst to different thinking as far as extended life of assets.

## 9.2.2   Compliance

One of the hardest things to do is to meet your regulatory compliance requirements. One of the challenges of the businesses is operating in 20 different regulatory regimes in 20 countries.

One of the strengths of TES is that we spend an awful lot of time and effort to ensure that we have everything in place so that we cover transboundary movements according to convention. We're probably the most audited and certified and permitted of the ITADs, particularly because of the recycling part.

We have enormous compliance and regulatory teams because strict compliance is our crown jewel from a competitive standpoint.

## 9.2.3   Conclusion

We are excited about Tess-amm's future with a large company like SK ecoplant, which has a strong focus on sustainability. As the world comes back from recent supply chain disruptions and as organizations look for financial as well as ecological sustainability, we will be working to finance, acquire, recycle, and refurbish its equipment.

# 9.3   Ingram Micro

*Todd Segers is the global vice president of ITAD & Reverse Logistics at Ingram Micro. He founded Green Asset Disposal, which merged with CloudBlue, which was acquired by Ingram Micro, which in addition to being one of the largest distributors of computer equipment in the world operates some of the most sophisticated processing facilities for disassembling and recycling electronics.*

I got started in technology in my mid-20s. In 1998 I was selling computer hardware and software for a large IT reseller called Insight based out of Tempe, Arizona. I was there until about 2002. `Insight.com` was mainly a hardware/ software reseller online. They wanted to start getting into the services business.

In 2002 Insight bought a company out of Chicago called Comark, which was basically a competitor, but they bought them more for their services arm. As we began the integration of the two companies, I joined the services group. I worked with their ITAD operations, which was part of their services arm.

I had never even heard about, or even thought about, the asset disposition business. I had always been focused on sell more, sell more, sell more. I came to realize what a valuable service it was.

At the time, I had a mentor who suggested that the massive buying of electronic gear in the lead-up to Y2K had flooded the market with used gear. I was seeing that at Insight.

So, Sergeant and I started an ITAD company in October 2003. I just sat in her front room and started making calls. We didn't have an operation at the time. I found other people who did, and I would sell the service and subcontract the work to them. My company was called Green Asset Disposal. We built it with a few other people but remained small.

So about 2008 or 2009, when the economy went downhill and the commodities markets dropped, it just wasn't a good time in the business. It was tough. So I reached out to one of our business partners, CloudBlue, which was one of our subcontractors that did the actual work. We sold our business to them.

I took over and led business development and sales for CloudBlue. We built the company up over the next three or four years and then sold to Ingram Micro in 2013. In 2015, the CEO of CloudBlue, Ken Buyer, took on a bigger role within Ingram Micro, and I took over global business development for the ITAD business for Ingram Micro.

We are purely ITAD services. We don't do refining and smelting. Yet we are probably one of the three largest IDADs in the world based on revenue. We send those materials downstream for refining, smelting, and ultimate disposal.

We process between three and a half to four million devices per year through our operations. That could be printers, PCs, laptops, or servers. About a year ago I took over the reverse logistics and repair division for our mobility group as well. We process one to one and a half million phones each year. All combined, probably four and a half to five million devices a year come through the facilities that I operate, both in the United States and internationally.

Repurposing and ESG have always been part of our DNA. I would say the social aspects came more to the surface as far as our core offerings and what we try to do for our employees and even the communities around where we operate. When we started this business in 2003, we called it Computer Asset, Remarketing, and Disposal (CARD). We rebranded to Green Asset Disposal around 2007.

We wanted to ride the environmental train. Green technology was growing back then, but data security has always been very important as was value recovery, but I think the resurgence interest in green technology and the ESG messaging over the last couple of years has been great for us, because of the environmental and governance of what we do in recycling but also repurposing devices in the secondary markets because devices do last so much longer now.

On the governance side, obviously you've got data security. Almost everything we have has data stored on it. Think about how many devices have batteries as well. We have to ensure that those batteries aren't getting thrown into landfills. We have to recover rare Earth minerals because there's only so many of them.

Our customers can use tools we provide or create their own for calculating carbon offsets for repurposed equipment. It helps them target a carbon-neutral goal. You enter all the devices—printers, PCs, laptops—and it will spit out this nice green report saying, here's your $CO_2$ emissions, avoidance, your water conservation savings, your air pollutant, diversion, etc. It's not a perfect science by any means, but it's really close. We provide a quarterly report on their environmental savings.

The funny thing is this industry hasn't changed a whole lot in the last 15 years. There's obviously some innovations around using newer technology as far as management of your business.

While the processes are not changing dramatically, one shift is to "as a service." In other words, organizations contract to lease equipment and then turn the equipment in on a regular schedule. They will no longer own the equipment, but the banks will.

One complexity that is being added into the mix is all of the IoT devices being deployed. They may have batteries and data in them. The spectrum of devices is going to grow exponentially, and we will incorporate processes to handle them.

Because banks are so heavily regulated, you'll see more and more people doing it right, driven by data security concerns. I don't think a whole lot is going to change. I think when you start looking at IoT and stuff like that and you think about the number of weird devices that have a battery and that have an IP address, and are storing data, you have a growing problem.

More and more corporations are getting better at tracking their assets. Some of our larger healthcare and insurance customers track their assets very well, but as you start working your way down in size, most companies don't have as robust asset management practices. I think ESG will drive the necessity for them to truly track where those materials are sitting and what they are.

Ingram Micro as a distributor of products wants to be aligned with new requirements in the EU and Latin America for manufacturers to take responsibility for recovering their product. If we're shipping hundreds of millions of devices out every single year, we will try to make sure we can take back as many as we can, but also partner with the OEMs to help them be a collection engine, to bring those back.

## 9.4  Summary

These three stories from industry pioneers gave you insights into the growing industry of IT asset disposition. It's an exciting field that appears to be consolidating as each of these companies has grown by acquisition and partnership. There will always be a geographic element to the industry. It's one thing for a manufacturer to be centrally located in China and depend on a global logistics network of container ships, trains, planes, and trucks to distribute its product to every location. It's another for an ITAD to collect all the devices from thousands of manufacturers when they are being disposed. There has to be distributed collection points, regional processing, and downstream facilities to handle the waste. Local regulations may be different and, even in the case of e-Stewards, explicitly bar the export of waste. This means there will probably continue to be thousands of ITADs and even more as more countries enact laws requiring responsible recycling and repurposing of used devices.

In the next chapter, we turn to the data sanitization requirements of the largest concentration of data storage devices: the data centers operated by large enterprises, colocation companies, telecom providers, and hyperscalers like Amazon, Google, and Microsoft.

# Data Center Operations

Data centers pose unique challenges for a data sanitization program. They typically hold many petabytes of data spread across thousands of servers and data storage systems. They often host systems for many different customers whose data has to be strictly segregated.

Data center operators have many tasks. They have to ensure that power and cooling and network connectivity are always available. They have to provide for physical security, which in a multitenant data center can involve locked cabinets, cages, or even segregated rooms. Visitors are checked in and out through man traps. In some instances, they are weighed on scales both on the way in and the way out to prevent theft of equipment.

Often data center operators are responsible for the physical maintenance of servers and storage arrays. This is where they can provide data erasure services, both for their customers' requirements and for maintenance and cost savings.

## 10.1    Return Material Allowances

Most data centers have strict data security policies, one of which is that a customer's data may not be removed from the data center without authorization. This poses a problem for the data center operators because they own and manage thousands of storage devices, usually in the form of removable hard drives that can be swapped out if they are being upgraded or are in need of replacement because of failures. Multiterabyte hard drives of data center quality are very expensive, up to $10,000 for a single drive. Typically the manufacturer sells them under warranty. A failed hard drive can be returned to the manufacturer under the returned material allowance (RMA) terms of sale to receive a replacement hard drive.

But how can a data center operator return a hard drive that onboard diagnostics says is getting ready to fail if their policy bars them from removing customer data from the data center? They can't, and this leads to high costs as the data center operator has to purchase new drives to replace failing drives even when they are still under warranty. Poke around inside a large data center and you are bound to find a pile of hard drives scheduled for degaussing or shredding. Keep in mind that placing a hard drive in a degaussing machine exposes it to strong oscillating magnetic fields. It will never be usable again, and the manufacturer will not accept it as RMA. It is destined for a landfill.

Data sanitization of hard drives provides a path to significant cost savings. Completely sanitizing a hard drive renders the hard drive certifiably erased, and thus it is able to be returned to the manufacturer.

## 10.2    NAS

Network-attached storage (NAS) is simply large arrays of hard drives, or in a modern data center, SSDs mounted in racks, that can be treated as a single storage system. They are typically configured in redundant mode (RAID) to protect from data corruption. They require continuous maintenance.

## 10.3    Logical Drives

Logical drives are data storage "drives" that look like a single hard drive to the operating system. Yet, the data is stored on a hard drive with other logical drives. A logical drive can span multiple physical drives across the data center. If, for instance, an organization wanted to keep all of its PII in the "same place," it could be recorded to a logical drive, which could then be erased in a single operation even though it spanned many physical devices.

Let's talk about LUNs. A LUN is a logical unit number. It's just a way to designate all the components of a data storage system that are grouped together to appear to be a single storage address. The "logical unit" is essentially a virtual device addressed by the SCSI, iSCSI, or Fibre Channel protocols. To the storage management system it appears as a single location even though the data could be written to tape drives or multiple hard drives spread all over the data center, even multiple data centers.

While LUNs can be used with any device that supports read-write operations, such as tape drives, they are most commonly used to refer to logical disks created on a storage area network (SAN). The term LUN is also (incorrectly) used to refer to the logical disk itself.

According to the MiniTool wiki, the LUN can reference the entire RAID set, a single drive or partition, or multiple storage drives or partitions. In any of these cases, the logical unit is regarded as a single device and is identified by the logical unit number.

## 10.4   Rack-Mounted Hard Drives

Erasing modern hard drives in a data center is not as easy as it may appear at first glance. You can't just have the OS systematically write zeros and ones to every sector on the disk. First, the disk controller may be keeping track of bad sectors and not allow you to write to them, even though a forensic tool can still read the data. Second, there are many components in a hard drive that store data that also have to be sanitized.

Firmware embedded in the hardware controllers for a disk drive can contain critical data including encryption keys. To improve storage and retrieval times there may be ranks of solid-state memory chips that cache data before it is written to the platters or as it is read.

A complete sanitization of a hard drive buried deep in the data center means that the software used has to reach out and not only overwrite the targeted disk sectors, but it has to know what kind of drive—from which manufacturer—the data is stored on. Separate drivers for each one have to be called so that all the firmware and cache memory can be reset too.

One large data center services company has a team of hundreds of technicians that are deployed to data centers around the world. Their purpose may be swapping out gear or diagnosing problems, or routine maintenance. If their task is to sanitize a particular hard drive, LUN, RAID, or an entire battery of storage in a NAS system, they must first know what model and manufacturer they are going to have to deal with. They can install the required image of the erasure software with the OS (usually a stripped-down version of Linux) to a thumb drive before traveling to the assigned data center. Once there, they insert the thumb drive in the relevant machine and issue the commands to erase the designated devices.

Creating software that has the specific work-arounds to erase all the components of each hard drive model is not an easy task. The software developer must have access to each manufacturer's technical documentation. Often they have to investigate a working device to discover the particular instruction sets needed. Then they have to test the software against the hard drive and complete a full forensic analysis to verify that it works. Every time a manufacturer releases a new model, or even a new firmware update, the software provider has to retest its erasure capability against the new or updated device. This is why simple OS operations or one-size-fits-all solutions like DBAN are inadequate for all but home use.

Erasing a large storage array can take many hours. It is a good idea to review the standard required before embarking on a seven-pass erasure of large amounts of data. Keep in mind that most modern storage devices can be effectively sanitized with a single-pass overwrite. The technicians may leave the data center altogether while the sanitization is underway. They return later to collect the thumb drives, which contain the record of the erasure including any errors reported such as failed sectors or a complete failure to erase. They can upload the erasure certifications to a tracking system to be accessed by the customer or used to create auditable reports of the sanitization records.

## 10.5   Summary

Cloud data center operators have taken distributed data storage to a new level. Files and drives can be replicated for backup and availability across multiple physical data centers. We like to think that data centers are going the way of mainframe computers yet in reality data centers are being transitioned to specialists, the so-called hyperscalers like AWS with 38 locations around the world, GCP (34), Azure (16), and, to a lesser extent, IBM, Oracle, Digital Ocean, and Rackspace. There are more than 100 companies with extensive networks of data centers that host services for others. With 310 data centers Equinix is one of the largest.

From the largest data handling tasks that are required in data centers in the following chapter we turn to the smallest task: file erasure.

# CHAPTER 11

# Sanitizing Files

## 11.1   Avoid Confusion with CDR

There is a bit of confusion about terms when it comes to *file sanitization*. After widespread attacks that spread via shared files that contained malware, the security industry responded with solutions that included tools that would strip the content out of a file and then reconstruct it into a new clean file. This is often called *file sanitization*. A Word doc or an Excel spreadsheet may be weaponized (the attack against RSA Security in 2010 was executed with such a spreadsheet). A file sanitization solution can be deployed at corporate gateways that look into a Word doc or a spreadsheet and extract the words, cells, and formatting; then it builds a new clean file with the correct extension. There are at least nine startups that have solutions for this, including SASA Software, Votiro, and YazamTech. Some of the earliest solutions were deployed in appliances that were located in the lobbies of corporate offices. An employee or visitor would insert a thumb drive into a USB port, and the file would be extracted, scrubbed, and put on an internal file server. Then the user could retrieve a safe file when they connected to the corporate network. To avoid confusion with file *erasure*, another term being floated is *content disarm and reconstruction as a service* (CDRaaS). This chapter is about erasing data in files.

## 11.2   Erasing Files

Think about the difficulty of applying data sanitization to files on a hard drive. A computer file could be a Word doc, a spreadsheet, a slide deck, a text file, computer code, output from an application, image, CAD/CAM, binaries, HTML, and hundreds of other file types. When a file manager stores a file, it records all of the metadata and substance on a hard drive. The driver for the storage device writes a string of ones and zeros, often using compression, to sectors on the platters or SSD. The file could be scattered all over multiple platters, with the computer keeping track of the order in which each chunk of the file is written and to where. When the file is retrieved to memory, it is rebuilt from all of the segments using the pointers created when it was stored. While a complete disk overwrite can systematically overwrite each disk sector, starting from the first and working through to the last, how can you overwrite a single file?

Modern operating systems use the concept of a trash bin. When a user or application "deletes" a file, it is merely designated as "trash." The actual file is not moved anywhere; the file management system just notes that it is trash and does not display the file in its original directory.

When you "empty the trash" on a computer, you are merely removing the pointers to the files so the file management system can no longer find the associated data to rebuild and present the contents of the files. The user, or a casual hacker, cannot see that the file even exists. The search function will not find either the filename or any of the data that was in the file. But, at least temporarily, all of the data still resides on the disk. The sectors on the disk that contained the file are freed up as they are marked as disk "free space." Subsequent saves of other files may or may not overwrite the original data. A simple forensic tool can be used to read all of the sectors on the disk and reconstruct the original file from the data it reads. You may have deleted that spreadsheet containing the day's transactions, including credit card information, but you did not remove the credit card numbers from the storage medium.

Some malware types specifically look for data residing in disk free space under the assumption that the owner wanted to get rid of the valuable stuff. The malware targets that for exfiltration.

Erasing critical data from a large data lake presents a similar problem. Think of Facebook attempting to comply with GDPR requirements to "forget" a user when they request that their account and all their data are removed. Facebook reportedly uses a system much like a trash bin. When one of its billions of users requests that their account be closed, Facebook moves all of their data to a collection of hard drives in a room set aside within one of its data centers. The user's access is terminated, and the data is held for 30 days in case the user has second thoughts and wants to revive their account. After 30 days the hard drives that have collected all the expunged accounts are wiped or destroyed. During that 30 days the assumption is that the original locations for the user's pictures, videos, comments, and profile have been overwritten.

A question to address before asking how to sanitize files is, when should you sanitize a file? We address both questions next.

## 11.3 When to Sanitize Files

One example of file erasure came up for a large building materials company when it was flagged in a corporate audit because the auditors found evidence in employee browser histories that employees were violating corporate policy by visiting inappropriate websites. While hiding evidence of a policy violation is counter to the whole point of an audit, and possibly breaks laws, the company was able to avoid future audit failures by ensuring that browser history files were thoroughly sanitized with software. Most organizations enforce browsing behavior with secure web gateways, which prevent a user from viewing the inappropriate sites, a much better method of enforcing a policy than auditing browser histories.

Deciding when to erase files comes back to the organization's data management policies. What types of data are allowed on corporate devices? Documents marked CONFIDENTIAL or SECRET? Company financials? Critical intellectual property like patent applications or design files? What about PII such as national identity numbers, health records, and credit cards?

Is there a data lifecycle requirement to destroy data after a predetermined length of time? Data retention policies are one of the most common reasons to find and erase files.

Part of an information lifecycle management system is the creation of a data policy that categorizes types of data and establishes whether a particular role is allowed to have it on a particular device. Then a data discovery tool can be employed to help enforce the policy. At the very least the discovery tool finds files by name and type and often will scan the files for the existence of critical data like PII. Data discovery tools can scan every endpoint and identify all file types, PII, browser history files, and cached web pages and images.

A desktop computer in a call center may have to retain customer information. But a portable laptop or tablet that could be stolen from an employee's vehicle or home should be treated differently.

To implement a data sanitization program at the file level, the organization has to decide what types of data can be stored on what types of devices. After content is discovered on a device that violates the data policy, a command can be sent over the network to sanitize it.

## 11.4  Sanitizing Files

Sanitizing a file requires overwriting. Each sector that contains segments of the file is overwritten with ones and zeros pursuant to the desired level of insurance against forensic analysis. A record should be kept of the erasure, preferably in a central location. The records should be tamperproof and auditable.

## 11.5  Summary

Because data centers have the largest volume of data and storage devices, they have the most to gain from data sanitization. The direct benefit is money saved thanks to taking advantage of RMA return policies. But the bigger benefit is in customer retention as the data center operator demonstrates their ability to protect their customer's data throughout its life.

In the next chapter we look into the unique challenges for data sanitization in the cloud where the fastest growth of data is occurring. Wearables, gaming, and sensors all report their data to the cloud. As licensed on-prem software evolves to software as a service, most applications will reside in the cloud generating and storing data.

# CHAPTER 12

# Cloud Data Sanitization

Cloud platform providers such as Amazon, Google, Microsoft, Rackspace, and hundreds of others of IaaS providers should all be able to document and demonstrate their own data sanitization processes. But keep in mind that security of data is a shared responsibility.

## 12.1 User Responsibility vs. Cloud Provider Responsibility

A cloud provider is responsible for the following:

- All hardware and physical security for hosting the data repository. The responsibility for hardware includes the requirements to properly sanitize storage media when it is being removed for upgrades or replacement.

- Licensing and ensuring software updates and patches are available for the operating systems, database solutions, etc., that they sell on-demand.
- Logging access.

The user of a cloud data service is responsible for the following:

- Discovering and classifying all data stores
- Setting access controls, privileges, and authorizations
- Monitoring access for malicious or unintended use, and compliance purposes
- Alerting on anomalous or malicious activity
- Building systems that allow the organization to respond rapidly and effectively to alerts
- Generating audit reports to demonstrate compliance
- Sanitizing data when a regulation or security concerns call for it

These user responsibilities need to be layered on top of the services a cloud provider enables. Third-party solutions for cloud data compliance and security should provide all these capabilities. The tools should be easy to deploy, be easy to use, and provide actionable intelligence to remediate breach attempts. They should also allow the fast generation of audit reports for all the scenarios: internal audit, regulatory audit, and civil court proceedings.

The safe handling of storage and compute devices that may contain customer data should follow the procedures described throughout this book. Ideally, a cloud provider will completely overwrite all storage before hardware is sent to a facility for responsible recycling.

Although not documented, observers of Facebook have postulated that it uses the following process when an account holder requests that their account be "deleted." Facebook maintains a vast amount of data on every one of its 2 billion+ accounts—every post, every "like," every image, every friend, every comment, conversation, and live stream. From a privacy perspective, Facebook's data is trove for intelligence agencies, hackers, and identity thieves. Even for an account meant to be anonymous, it is possible to rebuild the true identity of the account holder from the data that Facebook does not make public: geolocation, time of day, metadata of uploaded images.

When a user requests that an account be deleted, Facebook reportedly moves all of their data to designated drives located in a segregated area. The data is held there for 30 days in case the user wants to retrieve the data and reestablish their account. After 30 days, the physical storage medium undergoes data sanitization including overwriting and physical shredding. It is assumed that the storage medium is handled in an environmentally responsible manner.

## 12.2    Attacks Against Cloud Data

There have been no widespread attacks against the cloud infrastructure providers made public other than indications that the NSA attempts to tap into all the data that flows into them. The vast majority of successful breaches of cloud platforms has been due to lost or stolen credentials, often showing up in GitHub repositories, or the lack of access controls on S3 storage buckets. Most breaches reported by the popular press are actually exposures; a security researcher scans millions of S3 buckets, searching for large repositories of information that are exposed. When these are discovered, the researcher notifies the data owner (responsible disclosure) to give them a chance to protect the data. After the data owner closes the hole, the researcher invariably publishes a report detailing the number and type of records they discovered. This serves to reduce trust in the organization that had sloppy controls and could be damaging to their reputation. There is also the implied assumption that a bad actor could have discovered the store of data at any time, so there could have been a breach requiring disclosure to the impacted parties.

Other attacks against cloud infrastructure are possible and usually involve sophisticated side-channel attacks to access memory in an adjacent virtual machine hosted on the same microprocessor.

## 12.3    Cloud Encryption

The most complete and effective method of sanitizing data on physical infrastructure that is not owned by the organization is encryption. The term *zero trust* was originally applied to data stored in the cloud. When launched, data storage services like Dropbox, Box, Google Drive, etc., promised that a user's data would be fully encrypted on their service. But these services were responsible for that encryption and thus held the encryption keys. Because key management is complicated, most services use the same encryption keys for all customer data. This means the service provider and their employees could see all of the data. The risk of exposure was addressed by background checks and internal policies and procedures. A customer would have to *trust* the service provider to follow those procedures. The provider would trust its employees to follow its policies.

A zero-trust model for data storage means that all of the processes that rely on trust to work are eliminated by simply giving the customer the responsibility to encrypt their data and maintain their own keys.

Key management is the hard part of encryption. Applying algorithms to cleartext is easy. Just combine a key, a very large string of digits, with the cleartext, after the digits have been reduced to hexadecimal notation. The encryption key is generated from the product of two very long prime numbers. It is computationally extremely expensive to derive the two factors from the public key. Only the person with the two prime numbers can reverse the encryption algorithm to decode the encrypted data.

The following are the things that make key management difficult:

**Revocation** When a user is no longer part of an organization, the need arises to revoke their privileges. This means knowing exactly where the user's keys reside and effectively erasing them.

**Rekeying** If a key is suspected of being lost or stolen, it is necessary to generate a new key. All of the data encrypted by the compromised key must be decrypted and re-encrypted with the new key. Sometimes this is called *key rotation.*

**Perfect forward security** For cloud storage systems the data is often encrypted at the source application and uploaded to storage over the Internet. Sometimes the storage system does the encryption. When that happens, the system relies on SSL to keep the data safe during upload. An attacker may have access to the network connection used and record all of the traffic. Even though the traffic is encrypted, there is the possibility, sometime in the future, that either the SSL encryption algorithm is overcome by the advances in cryptanalysis technology or those keys are recovered or stolen. This introduces the need for perfect forward security (PFS). The keys are changed regularly, so that even if an attacker recovers a key used years ago, it cannot be used to decrypt the user's current traffic.

You can see that with PFS, rekeying, and revocation, there is a data management problem. The fact that the encryption keys could be the "keys to the data kingdom" justifies the investment in time and resources to ensure that keys are managed effectively.

## 12.4    Data Sanitization for the Cloud

The trouble with encrypted data is that you cannot perform operations on it. To a forensic analyst there is often little difference between encrypted data and random data. The vast majority of cloud computing is performed on cleartext, meaning that the data resides in memory where an attacker can view it.

Snapshots are records of the complete memory of a workload, be it a virtual machine or a Kubernetes container. These snapshots are taken frequently and stored. They may contain critical information such as credentials, PII, or user activity at the time. A data sanitization program should recognize the existence of these snapshots, and they should be scheduled for sanitization as soon as they are no longer needed.

The cloud providers are well aware of the need for effective data erasure. Amazon AWS follows a simple procedure to address one scenario. After a user decommissions a data block, in Elastic Block Store, for instance, the distributed volume spread across many physical SSDs is taken out of service. When those blocks are recommissioned for a new customer, they are wiped before making them available for storage purposes (see `itexamtools.com/how-azure-aws-google-handle-data-destruction-in-the-cloud`).

Private data may indeed reside in those SSDs and could be potentially discovered if the physical devices were accessed, but wiping before reprovisioning is deemed to save on wear.

## 12.5  Summary

Now that we have covered all the places data resides, it is time to turn to creating a process that encompasses all of that data throughout its entire lifecycle: a data sanitization program.

# Data Sanitization and Information Lifecycle Management

Managing data sanitization is a shared responsibility, just as managing data is. Practically everyone in an organization is involved in the creation of data as they write, measure, code, present, and communicate. The IT staff members deal with data every day as their applications collect and store it and their systems log data.

The first step to managing data sanitization is to recognize its importance. This may be driven from a compliance requirement dictated by your regional government or your industry sector regulator. It is far better to become aware of these requirements in the early phase of their enactment; often there is a public comment period that calls for your contribution. Another driver is becoming aware of the security implications of data that could become exposed when it leaves your control. One more is the legal requirements for data retention. Reducing the data that is archived can reduce the burden during an ediscovery process in a civil suit.

The worst way to discover the need for data sanitization is when data is leaked or stolen, a regulator comes knocking, or a civil suit lodges a "do not expunge" action.

## 13.1    The Data Sanitization Team

When first launching a data sanitization program, it is critical to involve all of the affected parties. This may include the chief privacy officer, chief risk officer, legal department, HR department, IT security, and developers. It is optimal for the effort to be led by the CEO, or directed by the board, if only to have the remit to do it properly.

While all of these departments should be included, the ultimate goal is to have a designated leader of a group of interested parties. This team will engage in the following actions.

## 13.2    Identifying Data

Identify all the types of data collected and stored. How is data created, and where does it reside? Are there third parties that process, store, and archive data? Are there rogue teams or projects, so called shadow IT, that are creating apps or using SaaS or cloud services to store data? A mature organization may already have an information lifecycle management process in place. This makes it relatively simple to create a data sanitization program by latching on to the end-of-life of data.

## 13.3    Data Sanitization Policy

Create a data sanitization policy. The policy template in the Appendix is a good starting place. A policy should identify how each type of storage media—tapes, hard drives, SSDs, flash memory, cloud storage—is sanitized. A critical component of the policy is the record keeping that will be used to demonstrate that data has been destroyed. That calls for an immutable (digitally signed) record of erasure or physical destruction for each data sanitization action.

The policy should be aligned with the various regulatory regimes with which an organization expects to demonstrate compliance. An auditor from the Federal Trade Commission will be looking for different things than one from a data supervisor in the EU.

The policy should also conform nicely with the underlying framework an organization has chosen, be it NIST, COBIT, ITIL, or ISO.

## 13.3.1    Deploy Technology

An important part of a data sanitization program is the selection and deployment of commercial software tools for logical erasure. Because logical erasure (software overwrites) occurs at the end of life of the data, it is often a neglected capability in large data management solutions, which tend to concentrate on the data discovery and classification stages. This means that managing a data sanitization program requires oversight and scheduling of erasure events that the data discovery tools identify. It is imperative that all "delete" functions in data management tools are carefully inspected. An additional tool may need to be incorporated so that storage media containing deleted files and data can be scheduled for data wiping.

## 13.3.2    Working with DevOps

A senior person from the application development team should participate in the data sanitization team. That person can carry guidance to the developers on how to incorporate data erasure and end of life for physical media into their plans. Going the other way, the DevOps leader can bring concerns to the team early in the development cycle that may call for creating new processes and procedures when a new data storage requirement is being considered.

## 13.3.3    Working with Data Security

The data security team should also be represented on the data sanitization team. The sanitization team can provide additional support to a project that calls for data encryption by reinforcing the need for good key management. For instance, every time keys are rotated, data meant for eventual erasure could be left out of the re-encryption process. That data will be encrypted with old keys that have been destroyed, making the data unrecoverable.

## 13.3.4    Working with the Legal Team

Because data sanitization has so many touch points with legal needs, there should be somebody from the legal team involved in data sanitization management. The chief counsel would be a good candidate to head up the team. The legal team will be called on to handle and execute requests for data retention during the discovery phase of a civil suit or a regulatory action.

Even before a civil suit is formally started, the suing party petitions the court to enforce a do-not-destroy order calling on all records to be retained. This is usually a very broad petition going back many years and covering as many data types as possible. The legal team pushes back as much as they can. They do not want a competitor or regulator to uncover information that may not pertain to the immediate purpose of the ediscovery—so called fishing expeditions. Regularly scheduled data sanitization procedures may have to be put on hold if data was already scheduled for destruction. An ediscovery platform can sequester the requested data and make it available to the investigating party. There may be several such legal proceedings happening at the same time, each with different requirements.

It is best for the internal audit team to work directly with the data sanitization team to determine what measure will be taken to make regular audits as easy and painless as possible. It can be disruptive to an organization for the audit team to invent new requirements at the last minute.

To imagine an effective audit process, think about an event like the theft of a server or loss of a laptop. If the data sanitization team can demonstrate that all critical data had been erased per policy and all working data was encrypted and the keys destroyed as soon as the device went missing, then the incident can be closed. No notification to a regulator or breach disclosure to customers will be required. Of course, increasing physical security measures to prevent such theft or loss in the future is still a good idea.

## 13.3.5   Changes

Like all management processes there must be flexibility to allow for exceptions. These should be well-documented.

There will also be new exposures of data that were not foreseen and thus not incorporated into the data sanitization process. New side channel attack vulnerabilities in the way VMs are deployed could be discovered. The latest SSD or hard drive products may be misconfigured by the manufacturer so that data encryption does not happen or is poorly implemented. Keys may be stored in a way that makes them easily accessible by forensic analysis. Data sanitization management teams must be prepared to modify their policies and procedures to accommodate new developments such as these.

## 13.4   Summary

A data sanitization policy serves many functions. It provides assurance to auditors that there is a process in place for sanitizing data at its end of life. Like many policies, it also provides air cover if the decision to sanitize data is questioned. That decision cannot be applied haphazardly. Sanitization decisions must be carried out according to policy and applied across the board.

# CHAPTER 14

# How Not to Destroy Data

Anyone who has had to deal with getting rid of an old computer or smartphone has felt the anxiety of what to do about the data. Even if you are passing a device down the line to a child, relative, friend, or charity, there will be some trepidation. How can you be confident that none of your data will ever be viewed by the new owner? This visceral awareness leads to imaginative methods of data destruction, most do not preserve the device at all. The most common is to hit the hard drive with a hammer. Here are a few more.

## 14.1  Drilling

A quick trip to YouTube will pull up many home videos of people destroying hard disks. A frequently videoed process is to remove the hard drive from a PC or laptop and drill through the case and platters. This is certainly effective. It is highly unlikely that a hard drive so treated will ever function again. The average dumpster diver is not equipped to retrieve data from platters that cannot be simply plugged into a computer and read from the file system. Even common forensic tools will not be able to read a hard drive that has been subjected to a drill.

There are three reasons drilling hard drives is not a good idea. First, it can be dangerous if the hard drive is not held down properly and the drill operator does not take precautions like wearing goggles or a face shield.

Second, it is environmentally irresponsible to create e-waste that is probably going to end up in a landfill when the device could still have a usable life. If left in its computer, the whole system would command a higher resale price.

Third, the data still exists on the platters. Although there are no public reports of a lab being able to read the data from a hard drive with a hole in it, there is a theoretical path to retrieving the data. A read head attached to the arm of a home CNC machine could be passed over the device, following the tracks, and the data recovered.

Imagine that a bitcoin wallet had been stored on the hard drive. If it contained even a few coins, valued at $20,546 each as of this writing (down from a high of $68,789!), extraordinary measures would be justified to retrieve them. The proposed method is easily within the capability of an intelligence agency.

### 14.1.1    Nail Gun

One example to be found on YouTube is a test of various pneumatic nail guns. The narrator had to use a powerful nail gun to penetrate the cover and the disk platters. It may even be more effective than drilling because the platters were considerably warped even when the nails did not pierce them.

### 14.1.2    Gun

Yes, people use hard drives as targets. Set them up on a shooting range and hit them and you have a fun way to destroy data. Don't do this.

## 14.2    Acids and Other Solvents

Subjecting a loose hard drive or mag tape to an acid bath or any strong solvent is another process sometimes used in extreme cases. It comes with its own hazards, not the least of which is the safe handling of so much caustic material. This is not recommended.

## 14.3    Heating

One of the authors attended a conference of ITAD operators. A presenter related a humorous anecdote. He was visiting a customer in South America. As they left the customer's office, he noticed a truck had pulled up outside a neighboring office building and set up a BBQ grill on the sidewalk. Thinking that a savory lunch was about to be served, he wandered over. To his surprise, people from the nearby offices were lining up with hard drives. The grill operators were roasting the hard drives over a charcoal fire to sanitize them!

## 14.4    Incineration

Perhaps sanitization by heating is an extreme case, but the incineration of storage media is a common practice. We mentioned the nuclear launch codes onboard submarines earlier. Magnetic tapes and SSDs are often incinerated. However, destruction in this manner is harmful to the environment because it releases noxious gasses from mag tapes and hardware into the atmosphere.

## 14.5    Street Rollers

Another method sometimes used to destroy equipment is to drive over them with a large vehicle or pavement roller. This is probably effective but hard to build into a documented data sanitization process. The final piece size of the broken platters may not conform to the destruction standards.

## 14.6    Ice Shaving Machines

The mechanical scraping of a DVD or CD is possible, and it might also be effective because someone is highly unlikely to recover data from the thin, curled shavings. Shredding followed by mixing is recommended. However, the ice shaving method is difficult to fit into a regular process of data sanitization.

# The Future of Data Sanitization

As data as well as security and privacy concerns grow exponentially, so does the need for effective data sanitization. The future of data sanitization will follow the path of data management, which evolved to address storage arrays, data warehouses, and today's data lakes. Platforms will be devised in conjunction with data discovery tools to safely overwrite data wherever it resides whenever it meets the criteria of a policy to do so. Cryptographic erasure will play an increasing role as data security and strong encryption are applied more broadly. As the number and variety of digital devices grows, so will the need for overwriting or physically destroying them before recycling.

Crafting an information lifecycle management program should take into account future technology that will change the way data is created, stored, and disposed of.

Storage media has undergone a consistent path to denser and denser storage. Cloud data storage requirements are growing exponentially. Technology vendors will develop tools for erasing data from these new devices. The hope is that the technologists devising new storage methods will take into account data sanitization measures to make erasure simpler, faster, and easier to verify.

If data sanitization principles continue to be adopted, they could be incorporated into information rights management (IRM) tools. These technologies apply encryption to make data accessible only to authorized users. Rights to edit, copy, and forward are assigned to authorized users and enforced by a cryptographic wrapper. Taking the next step of assigning a "time to live" to each document or dataset would trigger the destruction of encryption keys at a future time that would be in accordance with the data retention period. Hence, crypto-erase data sanitization will take place, and if done with bravura, an audit trail of the operation should also have been created.

Secure communications is a field on the forefront of data protection. Telegram, WhatsApp, and Signal are three such means of secure communications. These systems are great at encrypting "over-the-air" communication, but they have a vulnerability. Complete message transcripts reside on the devices of the parties communicating. Spyware surreptitiously installed on those devices could record the cleartext displayed on the screen (or the voice communication). Also, a law enforcement agency could commandeer the device and pressure the user to unlock it. A solution to that has been implemented by Signal called *ephemeral messages*. Much like Snapchat, the messages exist for only a short while; therefore, they would not be discoverable.

We also have to consider entirely new ways of storing data when we look at the long term.

Some technologies that have been proposed as the future of data storage are covered next.

## 15.1    Advances in Solid-State Drives

Solid-state chips are layers of silicon etched and doped to create memory locations. Conceptually, stacking many layers of silicon is easy to envision. Modern flash memory is manufactured with dozens of such layers providing for terabytes of data storage in a single chip. Samsung introduced a 1 TB chip containing 96 layers in 2019, and both Micron Technology and SK Hynix announced 176-layer NAND flash memory in 2020.

If chips were cubes instead of flat wafers, the storage density could be much higher. Instead of an array of dozens of chips on boards, as in a modern high-capacity SSD, a single cube could be used. One of the biggest hurdles to overcome will be heat generation. A flat device has much more surface area to radiate heat, whereas a cube would run very hot. Although the trend is toward more and more layers as well as higher bits per cell (up to four today), it is not likely that chips will be manufactured with enough layers to make them blocks of silicon. Other storage technology will most likely come to replace NAND SSD. Currently, it appears this technology could be pushed to store up to petabytes of data on a single drive.

## 15.2 Shingled Magnetic Recording

On modern hard drives, the write head is larger than the read head. SMR is a simple upgrade whereby each new track slightly overlaps the previous track, similar to shingles on a roof. The narrower read head can still read each track. This makes each track effectively thinner allowing for denser data storage. The drawback is when you want to overwrite the data and the fatter write head obscures adjacent tracks. To account for this, either on-device or operating systems' software manages the tracks in a way that is similar to block storage in SSDs.

Because data sanitization, in this particular case, means overwriting tracks, the entire append-only segment of tracks must be overwritten. This technology could theoretically push drive storage up to many terabytes per drive.

## 15.3 Thermally Assisted Magnetic Recording, Also Known as Heat-Assisted Magnetic Recording

The history of storage media is a constant push to denser storage and faster access times. One example is the need for storing video in Super Hi-Vision (SVH), which is pushing research into denser magnetic storage. To get high density, you need a smaller grain size for the magnetic material on a platter. The write head flying over the platter imparts a magnetic field to the particles in a small area that can later be read. But the smaller the grain size, the harder it is to impart a new magnetic state on them. This is the property of *magnetic coercivity*, the ability of a ferromagnetic material to withstand outside magnetic fields. Obviously, higher coercivity means it is hard to change the state of particles on a disk, so you need stronger magnetic fields[*].

---

[*]Thermally Assisted Magnetic Recording. Hirotaka Shiino, Osaka Station, Broadcast Technology no.40, Spring 2010.

Researchers have discovered that applying a localized heat source to the magnetic particles reduces their coercivity, making them easier to be over-written. Thus, thermally assisted magnetic recording (TAMR) hard drives have lasers that focus heat energy on the spot on the disk that is being written. Data densities of 1 TB per square inch are possible with TAMR. This would result in drives that could store 12 TB per platter in a 4″ drive.

Overwriting, and thus data sanitization, of TAMR drives will be similar to sanitizing today's hard drives. As long as the drive is in working condition, the overwrite process will be effective. There may have to be heat load balancing to avoid overheating sectors of the platters, which could add to the time to overwrite an entire drive. Drives with super high density such as TAMR might mean higher erase times unless the read-write speeds are proportionally faster.

One thing to consider is that degaussing of TAMR drives may be far less effective using today's degaussing devices. The higher magnetic coercivity is exactly the property needed to prevent a degausser from working. Perhaps a degausser will also be an oven. Standards will have to be tested to come up with required temperatures and thermal "soak time" before the degaussing operation.

## 15.4   Microwave-Assisted Magnetic Recording

An alternative solution to the problem of writing to smaller and smaller magnetic particles is the use of microwaves. Western Digital has created such a system using 20 to 40 GHz frequencies.

Think of all those tiny magnetic particles crammed together on a layer on a disk drive platter. To keep them stable and from interfering with each other, new materials with higher coercivity are used. But that high coercivity means it is hard to change the magnetic polarization of each particle. Researchers have discovered that by applying an oscillating field to the particles (spin torque), they induce a wobble in their state. Destabilized in this way, the magnetic write head can flip them over. Their magnetic coercivity is reduced, making it possible to write data on disks with much denser magnetic particles; thus, you get greater data density.

Toshiba claims to be getting ready to produce MAMR drives with 16-18 TB capacity. (See www.sciencedaily.com/releases/2021/03/210309114347.htm.) Like heat-assisted magnetic recording (HAMR), microwave-assisted storage will pose challenges for degaussing. The magnetic particles are so stable that they may resist the application of a strong magnetic field using today's degaussers. Using the onboard microwave write-head to overwrite the data may be the only way short of pulverizing or incinerating to sanitize MAMR drives. Crypto-erase will be another option with the usual warnings about longevity and verification.

## 15.5    DNA Data Storage

DNA is a double helix molecule made up of four nucleotides with the symbols A, C, G, and T. Scientists have been working on manufacturing and editing DNA strands for years, mostly for gene therapy. But similar techniques are being worked on to record and retrieve data in strands of DNA. Instead of the simple one and zero states available to current storage methods, there are four states to every position on a DNA strand, one for each type of nucleotide.

Teams funded by the Intelligence Advanced Research Projects Agency (IARPA) of the U.S. government, dubbed MIST, are working to develop the ability to write a terabyte of data to DNA and then read it, all within 24 hours. The current speed of adding a single nucleotide to a DNA molecule is one second, which is not yet a practical storage solution. A terabyte of data as we normally think of it is 8 billion bits and would need 2 billion nucleotides, which would take 63 years to write to DNA at that speed.

But the technology is attractive because the storage density is astounding. According to scientists at Los Alamos Laboratories, all data produced by humanity to-date could fit in a ping-pong ball–sized volume. (See `www.scientificameri can.com/article/dna-the-ultimate-data-storage-solution`.) All the data stored by Facebook could fit in a space half the size of a poppy seed.

Data sanitization for full datasets will be easy; just destroy the DNA by heating, mixing with chemicals, or irradiating. The challenge, if DNA storage ever becomes viable for commercial use, will be to locate and sanitize specific data while leaving the remaining data, as well as the storage itself, intact.

## 15.6    Holographic Storage

Using lasers to record and read data is the basis of CDs, DVDs, and Blu-Ray discs. The next evolution is the concept of holographic data storage where data is written into a three-dimensional volume. This technology has been demonstrated at data densities of 250 GB per cubic inch of media and can be accessed at the rate of 10 GBps (see `medium.com/codex/ the-laser-and-the-future-of-data-storage-ab5a44109c6`).

While holographic data storage (HDS) has not seen a commercial application because DVDs suffice for now, there is a hybrid data storage solution that is showing promise called 5D storage.

5D storage uses a laser to write into a special quartz glass disc infused with nano particles of gold and silver. It is three dimensional because up to 18 different layers have been demonstrated. The tracks are at different depths and contain different data depending on the direction from which they are read by the laser. The direction and polarization of the reflected light are the two additional "dimensions" to make it 5D.

The tremendous storage density of 5D disks—up to 360 TB in tests—is not the only intriguing property. The disks are stable up to 1,000 degrees C, and one group estimates that the lifetime of the storage medium is nearly infinite. (See `journals.aps.org/prl/abstract/10.1103/PhysRevLett.112.033901`.)

Thus, 5D storage is often proposed for long-term archiving of vast amounts of data.

While the technology for 5D was developed at the University of Southampton, the production of 5D disks was acquired by the Arch Foundation, which seeks to preserve data long term. It donated one of the first 5D disks to Elon Musk who placed it in the red Tesla that he sent into solar orbit on the first Falcon Heavy booster. The disk contains the Foundation Trilogy by Arthur C. Clarke. (See `www.southampton.ac.uk/news/2018/02/spacex-5d-crystal.page`.)

It is not yet reported if 5D disks can be overwritten. Much like DNA storage, until 5D storage can be overwritten, destruction will be the best way to sanitize 5D disks. Particle size will present a problem because of the data density, so pulverizing to dust will probably become the recommended practice. Melting quartz at 1,600 to 1,700 degrees C is possible too.

As long as decryption keys are not stored on the disk, crypto-erase is viable for storage media like CDs and DVDs. But a storage medium meant to be kept for thousands of years probably precludes relying on crypto-erase because the useful lifetime of practical encryption today is measured in decades, not millennia.

## 15.7    Quantum Storage

There is a growing expectation that quantum computing will be dramatically disruptive. Think of quantum computing as an upgrade to digital computing where every operation is done on binary bits. In quantum computing, the new bit is called a *qubit* and has more states than just on or off like a traditional transistor. Because quantum mechanics is at work, these states can represent anything between one and zero, denoted by a quantum vector.

The promise of quantum computing is that some operations such as factoring large numbers will be much faster. The implications are that today's encryption algorithms are threatened by quantum computing. Cracking large encryption keys is theoretically infeasible with today's computers. The time to factor the encryption key into its component primes (each more than 100 digits) is measured in decades, even with a supercomputer. Quantum computing could make factoring trivial, and thus anything encrypted today may be subject to decryption as soon as a practical quantum computer is built.

Note that the threat of quantum computing also threatens the effectiveness of crypto-erase.

Quantum computing is in its early stages of experimentation. The largest quantum computing devices developed by Google and IBM rely on Helium-3, a byproduct of nuclear research, and special superconducting cables available only from a single source in Japan. (See `technologyreview.com/2019/01/17/137811/quantum-computers-component-shortage`.)

Researchers are also investigating quantum storage technology. One approach is to use qubits for storage. Beyond that, most researchers are looking at ways to preserve the quantum states of photons. A photon has many properties that can represent data. Spin, frequency, orbital angular momentum, and entanglement are just four. Capturing and recording these states in crystals doped with rare Earth elements is one approach. Other techniques take advantage of the properties of ytterbium (Yb) or diamond.

None of the proposed quantum storage methods to date could be called non-volatile. In other words, the data is easily lost if the device loses power or the source of excitement of the photons.

That said, quantum computing holds the promise of generating huge data-sets. The output may not be stored in quantum states but rather transferred to traditional media.

In anticipation of widely available quantum computing in the near future, researchers are working on post-quantum encryption techniques. If they are used, the effectiveness of crypto-erase will be extended, but there is always the potential for advances in computing that may challenge crypto-erase as an effective means of data sanitization.

## 15.8  NVDIMM

Modern computing memory resides in DIMMs, those arrays of chips you will find in your laptop or on the motherboard of your server that make up system memory. Computers typically have 16 to 64 GB of memory (as opposed to the storage hard drives or solid-state drives) in dual in-line memory modules (DIMMs). These have replaced the single in-line memory modules (SIMMs) of more than a decade ago. The DIMMs contain all the data your computer needs to operate on as well as the applications that are loaded into memory. All of your spreadsheets, documents, presentations, images, and videos you are using are stored here while the computer is powered on. DIMMs are volatile memory in that when the power is off the data goes away.

Nonvolatile DIMMs (NV-DIMMs) are being produced to preserve data when the power goes off. This increases the speed at which the device can be restored to operation, which offers some advantages for enterprise computing. To accomplish this, regular flash memory modules piggyback on the DIMM along with a small power source that maintains the volatile memory long enough to record it on the flash memory.

With regular DIMMs, when a server, laptop, desktop, or tablet is powered off, the only data sanitization requirement is to access the storage on the device and overwrite it. With NV-DIMMs there will be the additional requirement to access another area where critical data resides. If you think about it, an attacker is going to be most interested in the latest files to be pulled into system memory, including credentials, certificates, decryption keys, and everything that was being worked on at the time of shutdown.

Typically, dynamic memory is not encrypted, so crypto-erase will not be an option for NV-DIMMs.

## 15.9   Summary

The future of data storage awaits us. It is just as hard for us to comprehend how much data will fit in a tiny space in the future as it was for Bill Gates to imagine why anyone would need more than 640KB of RAM in a home computer back in 1981. Maybe we will store data in implants in our brains allowing us all to have eidetic memories. (Will mortuaries be responsible for sanitizing that data before preparation for burial?) Wherever data storage leads, however many yottabytes (a yottabyte is 1,000 zettabytes), there will be concurrent need to sanitize data. The task of finding that data, classifying it, and scheduling it for sanitization will continue to be a problem for all organizations.

# Conclusion

There are thousands of privacy professionals and security practitioners whose days are consumed with concern for keeping data safe. They must think about how to keep it from prying eyes, ransomware gangs, spy agencies, and inadvertent leaks. In this book we have laid out a path for eliminating that concern, at least at one important stage of the data lifecycle—the end of its life.

There are myriad laws, regulations, and standards for data sanitization. But, thankfully, creating a data sanitization policy and living by it can fulfill all the reporting requirements for any of these as long as the guidance in this book is followed.

Perhaps the greatest result of publishing a book on data sanitization will be a single resource not only to promote good privacy and security but to move the world closer to a sustainable existence. We cannot stop the adoption of newer, faster, better technology, but we can reduce the waste associated with older generations of devices. Large manufacturers are beginning to take reusability into account in their designs. They already incorporate recycled materials in their products, and many take responsibility for returns and repurposing their products for a second life, or using the reclaimed materials for remanufacturing.

As related by the executives from TES, Ingram, and 3 Step, ITADs can grow their business by participating in sustainability. Initiatives from e-Stewards, I-SIGMA, and SERI are contributing to those efforts by standardizing practices. An organization can choose its e-waste recycling partner by reviewing the certifications of potential candidates.

Home users, perhaps, can start to feel confident that they can recycle their old broken laptops, tower computers, and those cell phones cluttering the junk drawer. Just knowing that their data will be sanitized before the device is resold may be enough to get them to finally de-clutter. They may even earn enough money from an older model to upgrade to the latest and greatest.

While the amount of data created will always grow at an ever-increasing rate, there is still hope that we can curtail the exposure of data in breaches and leaks by applying good sanitization practices. We can certainly contain the costs of data management by assigning an expiration date to it and ensuring that it is properly destroyed at the end of its useful life.

The demand for ever denser data storage with faster read-write speeds means that engineers are working away at new ways to store data. This book may help them think about the important aspects of data sanitization in their designs. It would be a disservice to release a new technology that was 10 times better than today's SSDs at storing data without ensuring that data erasure was at least 10 times better too.

Encryption everywhere would be a help, but keep in mind that encrypted data is incompressible. You may have a large but sparse dataset that is easily compressed into a small file. But once encrypted, all the blank or repeated patterns take up as much room as a fully populated dataset. Therefore, encrypted data takes up more space and would require more hard drives or SSDs or qbits to store.

In the world of cybersecurity, there is a little recognized virtuous cycle that leads to better and better security. It often appears that attackers have the upper hand with continuous success against ever stronger defenses deployed by organizations. What is really happening is that victims of cyberattacks are learning every day. There is no better "security awareness training" than experiencing a successful breach. You see it every day when your Facebook friends announce that they have been "hacked" and not to click or respond to any messages you may have received from them. What really happened was your friend used a simple-to-guess password and had not implemented Facebook's freely offered two-factor authentication, despite the hundreds of times you have told everyone you know to provide Google, Facebook, Twitter, and LinkedIn with your cell phone number so they can send a verification text when you attempt to log in from a new browser. After the embarrassment of having their account used to advertise sunglasses and the pain of recovering their account, your friend finally figures out how to prevent this from happening again. If they are smart, they will look at how to implement two-factor authentication for the other accounts they have.

Much like consumers, businesses experience the same cycle. Over the years they have enjoyed the benefits of digitization. They have computer inventory systems, and they have moved away from stand-alone equipment in a closet or data center to hosting in the cloud. They use email instead of the post and fax machines. All of these benefits should have been accompanied by proper security measures. By not investing in cybersecurity, they have accumulated security debt that will eventually have to be paid. That day comes when they experience a breach. In recent years, these have been very public because they involve ransomware. Not only is critical data lost, but operations come to a halt. Orders cannot be fulfilled. Email servers are down. All those digital improvements are inoperable.

This is when most boards and executive teams first become aware of their cybersecurity debt. They scramble to determine what they did wrong and how they can prevent this painful experience from ever occurring again. They bring in an incident response team to dig into the details of the breach. They hire a CISO who in turn hires a team. They start to scan their networks for vulnerabilities and schedule the updates to patch the most worrisome. They implement strong authentication. They deploy firewalls and shut off dangerous ports like telnet and RDP. They switch from antivirus to EDR solutions. Some recognize that they are targeted by state actors with unlimited budget and motivation to steal from them. These make the investment in a security operations center (SOC) that is staffed 24/7 and has the tools to identify and stop breaches before data can be exfiltrated. Others may decide to outsource their around-the-clock security to a managed detection and response (MDR) service provider.

Meanwhile, regulators see all the news stories about disruptions to supply chains because of successful attacks against critical infrastructure such as power grids, pipelines, communications, and transportation. They implement new laws and regulations requiring better security practices. In the case of GDPR, they may use ill-defined terms like *state-of-the-art security*, which does not help.

But regulations do provide air cover for organizations that are responsible to their stakeholders. The fines or additional regulatory oversight they may be subjected to justifies spending on compliance. So, industry sector by industry sector, companies get their own regulatory regimes that demand better security practices.

The same virtuous cycle will drive data sanitization practices. There will be constant improvement even though it may not lead to a reduction in news reports of lost, stolen, or exposed data. Exposure of consumer data has led to the creation of California 1386 (and then the California Privacy Rights and Enforcement Act of 2020), FACTA, GDPR, and dozens of similar laws around the world. Standards bodies such as SERI, ISO, and the IEEE are busy creating better guides to data sanitization. Even books are being written to help organizations implement best practices in data sanitization. The cycle will continue as new industry sectors discover they have a data problem. First the breaches will make them aware of it, and then the regulators will add urgency. They will invest in better data management, discovery, classification, and, ultimately, effective erasure.

Sustainability has its part to play too. ESG regulations are requiring the "right to repair" and imposing new guidance on recycling. Both of these need data sanitization to be effective. Reusing devices saves energy in manufacturing and transportation and reduces waste that is destined for a landfill. Just as privacy regulations intersect with cybersecurity requirements, ESG touches on information technology practices. Thus, all three—privacy, security, and sustainability—have their part to play in driving data sanitization forward.

Use this book to guide your own data sanitization practices. The following appendix includes a template for creating a data sanitization policy, the first step in your journey. It was first created by the International Data Sanitization Consortium (`datasanitization.org`), a great resource for practitioners.

The R2 requirements for data sanitization are included in "R2v3 Article 7: Data Security" in *The Sustainable Electronics Reuse & Recycling (R2) Standard* by SERI (2020).

Wherever you are in your journey, from just beginning to discover the need for data sanitization to already having processes in place, there will always be room for improvement and contributing to the definition of best practices in data sanitization.

# Enterprise Data Sanitization

# Policy

## Introduction

The purpose of this policy is to achieve compliance with regulations, specifically data protection laws, such as EU General Data Protection Regulation (GDPR), PCI DSS requirements, industry recommendations, ISO standards, and internal policies. This policy also serves to minimize the impact of data breaches and the associated loss of data. It also pertains to environmental and social, governance (ESG), where data sanitization assists in the overall targets for contributing to sustainability and the circular economy.

This policy targets both asset lifecycle recommended procedures and data lifecycle management procedures, with reference to data sanitization in the form of data erasure.

## Intended Audience

The responsibility for data protection and applying this data sanitization policy resides with and is primarily for data protection officers (DPOs) or chief information officers (CIOs), chief data officers (CDOs), chief information security officers (CISOs), chief technology officers (CTOs), IT managers, and those with responsibilities related to digital data.

## Purpose of Policy

To minimize the organization's risk exposure from data breaches, it is vital to assess the information lifecycle within the business in parallel with analyzing and documenting the asset lifecycle. The following examples should be added to documented work processes and taken into consideration to actively improve data protection.

## General Data Hygiene and Data Retention

Data erasure for files/folders is part of overall data maintenance, ensuring that redundant data isn't stored unnecessarily, which can increase IT costs and the potential for data loss and data breaches. Data retention policies should be mapped against data sanitization processes at the end of the retention period to avoid losing control of managed data.

## Data Spillage

Sensitive data can be inadvertently copied to an unauthorized system or application. That data should not just be deleted but thoroughly erased.

## Handling Files Classified as Confidential

In cases where an employee receives and handles confidential data on a PC temporarily, that data should without delay be securely erased from the system to prevent potential data leaks. An automatic routine to securely erase the recycle bin regularly is one way to enable easy implementation. Granular policies to securely erase specific file types by revision number and time stamp can also be implemented.

## Data Migration

Whenever data is moved from one location to another—from a retired server to a new server, or from one virtual machine to another—the original data location must be erased. Erasure is necessary for LUN reuse in a hosted environment when a user migrates to a larger LUN or leaves the cloud so that the LUN can be safely reassigned to a new user. This is true for both physical servers using

LUNs as storage and for VMs with dedicated storage on a particular LUN. This complies with ISO27018.

## End of Life for Classified Virtual Machines

Many organizations manage virtual machines that are used by a line of business for a particular project that covers a specific period of time. When the project is completed, the data deletion should not be the primary precaution taken. Instead, it should be completely erased. Targeted erasure of a VM is necessary when the VM is deleted or changes location in the data center. You should be able to achieve this without rebooting the host. By installing the erasure solution at the VMware ESXi level, you can manually erase VMs in VMware vSphere. All files associated with the targeted VMs should be erased, including VMDK, VMSD, VMX, and VMXF.

## On Customer's Demand

This could address a business-to-business partner that wants to terminate the relationship and requires that their data be securely erased with an audit trail after end of contract. Most NDAs stipulate this.

Also, in jurisdictions such as the EU, "right-to-be-forgotten" rules dictate that if consumers ask you to remove their data from your servers, you must comply. It is not enough to simply delete the record. Instead, it must be completely expunged without any possibility of coming back to haunt them. An audit trail with a certified report must exist to prove that the erasure occurred.

Temporary data: for example, after a disaster recovery exercise, there may be complete copies of data repositories saved to temporary storage. During major disasters, data is typically recovered from an off-site location. The same is true during disaster-recovery exercises, where real customer data is typically used in the test. Because of this, it's critical to erase the data from the secondary site. In either case, once production systems are restored, any data left on recovery disks should be erased. This could also apply to "test exercises" or similar when real data is being used.

## Seven Steps to Creating a Data Sanitization Process

The National Institute of Standards and Testing (NIST) outlines seven steps to creating an overarching cybersecurity framework. These steps are also applicable to creating a comprehensive data sanitization process.

## Step 1: Prioritize and Scope

The company recognizes the risks associated with lack of control over information throughout its lifecycle and further recognizes the need for an information lifecycle approach that entails proper data sanitization processes across each step. Particular information stores and applications are identified that fall within the scope of this policy. Resources are dedicated to data sanitization as this policy is implemented. The scope of the program is decided, starting with the highest priority information. Types of information that could fall within the scope include the following:

- Employee records (healthcare, performance, disciplinary actions, financial)
- Customer records
- Email and other corporate communications
- Legal documents (contracts, MOUs, public filings)
- Transaction records
- Intellectual property (patents, notes, research records)
- Marketing material
- Customer support documentation
- Manufacturing quality documentation

## Step 2: Orient

Once the scope of the data sanitization program has been determined for the business line or process, the organization identifies related systems and assets, regulatory requirements, and overall data exposure risks. This data audit will encompass all types of data collected, stored, processed, archived, and disposed of. The organization then identifies threats to, and vulnerabilities of, data stores, systems, and assets used to process that data.

## Step 3: Create a Current Profile

Map the status of existing processes with supporting documentation. Determine, where required, the appropriate method of data sanitization.

For example, map the process by which new customers are onboarded and how records are created and maintained as their orders are fulfilled, delivered, invoiced, and payments accounted for. As the records age, how are they archived? For how long? Is there a record retention policy for each regulatory environment? What is the appropriate procedure for disposing of those records at the end of their life?

## Step 4: Conduct a Risk Assessment

Identify the risk of regulatory action, including fines and oversight, imposed by regulators based on the current profile. Then, quantify risk to the organization deriving from improperly disposed of data including loss of IP, breach notification costs, and impact on brand and customer satisfaction.

## Step 5: Create a Target Profile

Goals for data sanitization management are established.

The target profile is the desired end state: a fully implemented data sanitization program within the scope defined in step 1. For each prioritized class of information its end of life (retention period) is defined, and appropriate data sanitization applied. For most information, that will entail certified software overwrites or crypto-erase, but some equipment may have to be physically destroyed and documents of that destruction maintained.

## Step 6: Determine, Analyze, and Prioritize Gaps

Determine what technology, processes, and people are required to move from the current profile to the target state. For instance, it may be determined that there is no process in place for permanently sanitizing temporary files such as those generated by browsing activity. A plan is put in place to deploy client software that can automatically sanitize temporary files. Another example of a gap may be the way hardware in a data center is returned to the manufacturer for warranty. A full disk sanitization process will need to be put in place to close this gap.

## Step 7: Implement Action Plan

Systematically work to close gaps and continuously improve data sanitization practices. Create measurable milestones and revisit the scope stage at least annually.

# Data Sanitization Defined

Data sanitization is the process of deliberately, permanently, and irreversibly removing or destroying the data stored on a memory device to make it unrecoverable. A device that has been sanitized has no usable residual data, and even with the assistance of advanced forensic tools, the data will not ever be recovered. There are three methods to achieve data sanitization: physical destruction, cryptographic erasure (crypto-erase), and data erasure.

# Physical Destruction

The process of shredding hard drives, smartphones, printers, laptops, and other storage media into tiny pieces by large mechanical shredders or using degaussers.

## Degaussing

A form of physical destruction, whereby data is exposed to the powerful magnetic field of a degausser and neutralized, rendering the data unrecoverable.

Degaussing can be achieved only on hard disk drives (HDDs) and most tapes, but the drives or tapes cannot be reused upon completion. Degaussing is not an effective method of data sanitization on solid-state drives (SSDs).

## Pros and Cons of Physical Destruction

Physical destruction is an effective method of destroying data to render the data unrecoverable and achieve data sanitization. Physical destruction can be harmful to the environment and destroys the assets so they are unable to be reused or resold.

# Cryptographic Erasure (Crypto-Erase)

Cryptographic erasure is used interchangeably with crypto-erase. Cryptographic erasure is the process of using encryption software (either built-in or deployed) on the entire data storage device and erasing the key used to decrypt the data. The encryption algorithm must be at a minimum of 128 bits. While the data remains on the storage device itself, by erasing the original key, the data is effectively impossible to decrypt. As a result, the data is rendered unrecoverable and is an appropriate method to achieve data sanitization.

The encryption on the storage device must be turned on by default, providing access to the API call to the storage device to remove the key, which allows cryptographic erasure to be supported.

Cryptographic erasure must verify the encryption key has removed the old key and replace it with a new key, rendering the data encrypted using the previous key unrecoverable.

The cryptographic erasure software will produce a tamper-proof certificate containing information that the key has been successfully removed, along with data about the device and standard used.

## Pros and Cons of Cryptographic Erasure

Cryptographic erasure is an effective and quick method to achieve data sanitization and is best used when storage devices are in transit or for storage devices that contain information that is not sensitive. Cryptographic erasure relies heavily on the manufacturer where implementation issues could occur. The users also could impact the success of cryptographic erasure through broken keys and human errors. But most important, cryptographic erasure still allows for the data to remain on the storage device and often does not achieve the regulatory compliance requirements.

## Data Erasure

Data erasure is the software-based method of securely overwriting data from any data storage device using zeros and ones onto all sectors of the device. By overwriting the data on the storage device, the data is rendered unrecoverable and achieves data sanitization.

Data erasure software does the following:

- Allows for the selection of a specific standard based on your industry and organization's unique needs

- Verifies that the overwriting methodology has been successful and has removed data across the entire device or target data (if specified)

- Produces a tamper-proof certificate containing information that the erasure has been successful and written to all sectors of the device, along with data about the device and standard used

Block erase can be a feature, but it is often used interchangeably with data erasure. Block erase is the ability for vendor software to target the logical block addresses, including those that are not currently mapped to active addresses, on the storage device to erase *all* data on the device. However, if the block erase software does not provide for the three steps noted in the data erasure definition, it does not achieve data sanitization.

## Pros and Cons of Data Erasure

Data erasure is the highest form of securing data within data sanitization because of the validation process for ensuring that the data was successfully overwritten and that the auditable reporting is readily available. Data erasure also supports environmental initiatives while allowing organizations to retain the resale value of the storage devices. However, it is a more timely process than other forms of data sanitization. In addition, data erasure forces organizations to develop policies and processes for all data storage devices within an organization.

## Equipment Details

Examples of technical equipment as part of managing the asset lifecycles within the organization include the following:

- Personal computers
- Laptops
- Tablets
- Servers
- Storage systems
- Photocopiers
- Network printers
- Network fax machines
- Routers
- Switches
- Firewalls
- Proxy filters
- Network-attached storage (NAS)
- Point-of-sale (POS) equipment
- Barcode readers
- Mobile phones
- Smartphones
- Removable memory devices (e.g., USB memory sticks or hard drives)
- Loose drives from any of the above

The following are examples of data media:

- CDs
- DVDs
- Backup tape
- Hard drives
- Solid-state drives
- Thumb drives
- RAM/ROM chips in devices

This rule applies to the following situations (nonexhaustive list):

- End-of-life disposal
- Re-deployment within the company (staff leaving or being reassigned)
- Maintenance work outside of the company premises
- End-of-lease return of equipment
- Warranty claims/returned material authorization (RMA) returns
- Service claims

## Asset Lifecycle Procedures

Asset lifecycle procedures are developed to ensure digital data is adequately protected from unauthorized disclosure when technical equipment or data media is being redeployed within the company, disposed of (end of life), or in any other way is leaving the company's or a third-party partner's physical control. The latter can include off-site service, for example, or RMA from the manufacturer.

This type of equipment contains data, sometimes being proprietary, classified, company confidential, personal, or otherwise of a sensitive nature, as well as software that carries license restrictions.

Before a change of control may take place, all technical equipment capable of storing or processing COMPANY data must use data erasure. This can be completed within the company's IT department, or a selected partner can also facilitate data erasure during the change of control. These selected partners include leasing companies that own the equipment, outsourcing partners that own or manage the equipment, or a professional IT asset disposal company (ITAD) that is contracted for their services.

With these security measures in place, the goal of the policy is to improve ITAD company procedures for encouraging reuse of equipment, within the organization or by new users outside the organization. The company policy is to minimize impact on the environment from equipment extending its life through reuse, donation, or parts usage. The following facts from a UN report are examples of information behind this policy and viewpoint:

- Lifecycle energy use of a computer is dominated by production (81 percent) as opposed to operation (19 percent).
- Computer use of a computer is dominated by production (81 percent) as opposed to operation (19 percent).

## Suggested Process, In Short

All technical equipment capable of storing or processing company data must use data erasure by a certified and approved data erasure software vendor before change of control may take place. The process should allow for full documentation and traceability, so, for example, an individual hard drive can be proven to be erased properly if questioned. This follows ISO27001 recommendations.

## Create Contract Language for Third Parties

The requirement for data erasure of equipment not owned by the company must be covered by a legal contract with the equipment provider. Equipment or data media that cannot be securely erased may require physical destruction.

More details for implementation of this policy are available in the following sections for reference purposes.

## Data Erasure Procedures

An effective data sanitization program requires that data erasure and verification processes are defined for each category of data and each type of storage media. This section should be updated as new categories of critical data are identified and new types of devices are introduced into the environment.

### Responsibility

The process owner is responsible for validating that the result of the data erasure procedures meet the requirements set out in this document. Validation of data erasure procedures should occur annually, at a minimum, or whenever new technical equipment type or data media type is introduced. The validation process should be documented.

If a service provider is contracted to perform the data erasure procedure, full traceability should be required and validation of this work needs to be carried out by the company annually, at a minimum.

As the process owner, external regulations or legislation may require specific procedures to be developed within a business process. Examples of this could be PCI DSS requirements for the safekeeping credit card information and data protection legislation to prevent the unauthorized transfer or processing of personal data.

## Validation of Data Erasure Software and Equipment

All data erasure procedures should be validated to meet the requirements stated in this document. Validation should rely on external certifications and approvals of software and equipment used for data sanitization. External certification and approval authorities should be organizations such as government certification authorities, national defense organizations, and those authorized to perform tests and grant approvals for Common Criteria. Internal tests based on thorough analysis of erased media are also approved, if thoroughly documented and performed to meet industry standards.

Damaged storage devices or data media should be subject to a risk assessment to determine whether they should be destroyed, repaired, or discarded.

Data erasure used on technical equipment or data media needs to be logged for future reference, maintaining an audit trail.

In the case of leased technical equipment, the legal contract must cover these data erasure requirements. The following factors must be considered:

- Does a validated data erasure procedure exist for the specific type of equipment or media involved?
- Is the equipment or data media defective and data erasure prohibited?

In general, there will be a need for data erasure when:

- Data changes location, leading to a change of owner control of the device.
- The device leaves the company's premises.

## Personal Computers

For most PCs (laptops or desktops), it is not necessary to physically destroy the hard drives, as long as they have successfully passed the data erasure process. A PC could be considered to have successfully passed data erasure if the procedure used can be validated to remove data from all addressable parts of the storage device.

Redundant PCs being disposed of, sold, or donated should complete data erasure to this standard before leaving the company control.

## Servers and Server Storage Systems

Servers and server storage systems hold large volumes of data from a variety of sources. A separate data erasure procedure must be implemented for each type of storage system (e.g., NAS, SAN) and hard drive technology (e.g., RAID level, SCSI, ATA, SATA) in use. Data erasure can take place on a drive level or logical level (LUN-level).

Note that for loose drives, data erasure is necessary for sanitizing disks outside the host, as is true with loose drives from storage area networks (SANs). Because of the chain-of-custody concerns, local data erasure of disks is necessary. Erasing loose drives requires an external host/boot device and connectivity between the drives and the host. Data erasure on failed disks removes the content so the drive can be transported to the OEM for warranty replacement. The data center, not the OEM, is responsible for data erasure.

## Photocopiers, Network Printers, and Fax Machines

Photocopiers are typically networked and many double as network printers. Any photocopier, network printer, or fax machine that contains a hard drive is likely to hold sensitive data. While this information is not readily available to end users of the machines, it is potentially available to maintenance staff. All such machines must therefore use data erasure before they leave the company for maintenance, disposal, or replacement. Any removal or replacement of the hard drive must be controlled and the procedures properly adhered to. These devices should use data erasure when being repurposed within the company to prevent data from being exposed interdepartment.

## Mobile Phones, Smartphones, and Tablets

All mobile phones (cell phones) may potentially contain sensitive information that needs to be securely erased before change of control takes place, especially models with advanced level of functionality (e.g., smartphones). Where business communication is likely to have taken place, mobile phones must always use a data erasure procedure. For mobile phones with SIM cards, all SIM cards must be removed before disposal and have data erasure performed on all memory cards that may reside in the unit.

## Point-of-Sale Equipment

In many cases, POS equipment is leased, and the requirements of data erasure should be addressed in a legal contract. If owned by the company, similar procedures as used for personal computers or servers should be used.

## Virtual Machines

When a virtual architecture takes advantage of elastic computing (expanding compute resources on demand), a process should be in place to ensure that no data is left behind when a VM is decommissioned, especially in public clouds.

## Removable Solid-State Memory Devices (USB Flash Drives, SD Cards)

When using removable memory devices, deleted files can be recovered. Files on SD cards that have been reformatted using a Microsoft Windows Format function, for example, or because the card's filesystem has been corrupted may be recovered. Software overwrites that overcome the inherent protections of SSD memory should be used. Each device should then be tested to ensure the data sanitization occurred and a record kept.

## CDs, DVDs, and Optical Discs

The only approved solution to achieve data sanitization on CDs, DVDs, or other types of optical disks is physical destruction.

## Backup Tape

The only approved solution to achieve data sanitization on backup tapes or other types of magnetic tape media is physical destruction or degaussing.

# General Requirements for Full Implementation

## Procedure for Partners and Suppliers

Units should make sure data sanitization procedures are also adopted by subcontractors, suppliers, or partners that handle part of the company's data.

When implementing these requirements, management is also recommended to exercise due diligence of the other party. Due diligence for this case could include the following:

- Reviewing an independent audit of the company's operations and/or its compliance with this document

- Reviewing and evaluating the disposal company's information security policies or procedures

- Taking other appropriate measures to determine the competency and integrity of the potential information management in the company

## Audit Trail Requirement

The following minimum requirements should be met for software performing data erasure. The data erasure software must be documented to state the successful completion of the process, and it must include the following:

- The equipment or data media serial number or erasure target name or path

- The erasure standard used

- A tamper-proof certificate that the erasure has been done correctly

- An effective system for managing audit trails in high volume and over time

## Policy Ownership

The normal procedure is that the CIO or CISO delegates the ownership of this data erasure policy to the internal IT security team. Tasks include the following:

- Ownership of the policy document

- Coordination of suppliers

- Overseeing the updates of internal, existing statements of work such as data sanitization processes and the enabling of internal and external audit processes

Each operational team identified as a process or asset owner in this policy should have documented workflows and responsibilities.

## Mandatory Revisions

This document does not claim to cover all possible technical equipment or data media that the company could possibly use to store or process data. Yearly revisions are recommended to update policy.

# Roles and Responsibilities

## CEO

The chief executive must recognize the requirement for a data sanitization policy and provide for the resources required to implement it. The CEO should review the scope and gap analysis and approve the implementation of the action plan.

## Board of Directors

The board of directors should ask for periodic updates and ensure that the corporate risk committee is part of the process.

The creation, implementation, and management of the data lifecycle management policy should be overseen by an executive who can report on a regular basis to the CEO and board.

Data architects must provide a plan consistent with this policy for classifying, discovering, protecting, and sanitizing all data. They should ensure that technology and processes are in place to fulfill these requirements.

# Index